SIMPLE TIPS FOR EFFICIENCY IN MANAGEMENT

N. RAMANADHA RAO

Foreword by

Dr. Y.P. ANAND

Director, National Gandhi Museum, Rajghat, New Delhi
(Former Chairman, Railway Board)

GYAN

GYAN PUBLISHING HOUSE

NEW DELHI-110002

SIMPLE TIPS FOR EFFICIENCY IN MANAGEMENT
(*Management*)

ISBN : 81-212-0582-4

Published in 1997 in India by

Gyan Publishing House
5, Ansari Road
New Delhi-110 002

Laser Type Setting at M.S. Printers, New Delhi
Printed at Mehra Offset Press, New Delhi

SIMPLE TIPS FOR EFFICIENCY IN MANAGEMENT

This book is dedicated to the memory of

SRI M.A. MURUGAPPAN

(the late Managing Director of The Coromandel Engineering Company Ltd.)

who was very much liked and admired for his qualities of head and heart.

His management policies bore a human face, always.

Contents

Foreword

Shri N. Ramanadha Rao's 'Simple Tips for Efficiency in Management', is true to its title. In twenty articles, written at different times during his long and distinguished professional career, he deals with varied subjects of wide interests in public and private sector management. In these articles, he recounts and analyses the most usual of the failures, failings and frailties of managers at various levels and offers simple and straight-forward but solidly practical guidelines to overcome major deficiencies and improve efficiency in the management of enterprises and departments. Though, as an Engineer, his emphasis is relatively more on projects and production units, he handles with equal ease and knowledge the other topical issues such as those of Marketing and Sales, Relations with Staff and Workers, Communications and Public Relations, and Pollution and Accidents.

He drives the truth home through simple real life incidents, anecdotes and proverbs collected during his long professional life. His emphasis is on right attitude, consideration for staff, customers and others, and concern for the righteous path. He is not the one to emphasise the 'killer' instinct or runaway profits by any means. Instead, he opts for business practices informed by the spirit of enterprise combined with social awareness. His approach is cooperative and the language simple and expressive. He would find no conflict between making profit and social well-being. Shri Rao's articles leave the reader with a happy and lasting impression that success and nobility in management are complementary virtues.

The book should inspire both the working and the intending managers to adopt efficient and effective as well as clean, open and fair management practices. Shri Rao deserves to be complimented for this highly useful and practical compilation on management.

Dr. Y.P. ANAND
(Director, National Gandhi Museum,
Rajghat, New Delhi)
(Former Chairman, Railway Board)

New Delhi,
29-7-1997

Preface

The subject of "Management" has acquired a great importance in the last few years. Managers are being entrusted with a vital role in our country's developmental activities. I sincerely believe that they could play their part better and more efficiently., if they get some information about the experience and views of their predecessors in this field.

With this in view, I have written this book. I hope that the Managers in Private and Public sector companies as well as the officers in the Government departments would find the contents of this book not only interesting but also quite useful. I also expect that the students in the Management courses too would benefit considerably by reading this work.

Rather than dwelling on the theories of management, I have given a few practical tips for improving the attitudinal aspects of the Managers. I have also dealt with a few subjects like "Standardisation" and "Pollution control in towns and cities" which are, in my view, allied to the subject of "management".

I shall consider that my effort is not in vain if this book could spur the Managers to do something to set right the ills and to improve the conditions in the society and to take the country on the path of progress to achieve the goal of prosperity and universal happiness of the people.

N. RAMANADHA RAO

1

Managers – Their Tasks and Hurdles in Their Path

A Manager is required to manage a situation ensuring the optimum use of the resources at his disposal. He has to solve the problems as and when they arise. His duties include assignment of work to and getting the work done by the staff working under him. His efficiency is judged by the results produced by him.

Managers are required in many fields like 'Finance', 'Personnel', 'Administration', 'Public Relations', 'Marketing', 'Project implementation', etc. A Manager's duties are multifarious, encompassing all the activities within his department. At times, a Manager has to tackle several departments, depending on his position and the type of organisation in which he is employed.

A Manager's role is neither like a science in which a result can be predicted with reasonable accuracy for a given data of the process and inputs, nor like an art in which the skill of the person can be depended upon for achieving a particular goal. It is indeed too complex for a simple definition. His success or failure depends on many factors like the circumstances, the people to be dealt with, the resources available and the expectations of the employer. It is just not enough if he has knowledge and is efficient in doing a work, individually by himself. For producing desirable results, he should be able to motivate and inspire the people working under him to give their best performance and to co-ordinate their efforts for achieving the objective set before them.

A Manager should be always conscious of three things in his work. They are 'time', 'resources' and 'human relations'. If a work is done taking, say, six months when it was reasonably expected to be done within three months only, the Manager may not have reason to be satisfied with himself. Nor could he expect any appreciation from others. Similarly, if an assignment is completed by spending two lakhs of Rupees or other resources equal to that sum when the same could have been completed with half of that expenditure, once again the Manager could not be rated high in his efficiency. Another Manager may complete these assignments within three months and spending one Lakh of Rupees only. But, if he treads on the toes of the people he dealt with in the process, his organisation would lose considerably more in the long run by way of loss of goodwill.

Many examples can be quoted of persons who have earned a great name as Managers in some organisations after having failed miserably in similar roles in some other organisations earlier in their careers or vice versa. This is attributable to the variable factors in the different problems they had to tackle.

Let us take an example of a Manager heading the Personnel Department in a Manufacturing Company 'A'. This organisation is running with a good margin of profit. The workers are by and large, disciplined and well trained in their work. The Management of the Company is progressive and fair minded. It gives a free hand to the Personnel Manager in the negotiations with the workers' unions. From time to time, the demands of the workers like 'raise in salaries', 'bonus and perks' and 'congenial working conditions' are conceded to a reasonable extent. Therefore, there are hardly any strikes worth mentioning and industrial peace prevails for several years.

Naturally, the Personnel Manager quite justifiably earns a reputation for his efficiency. Suppose at this stage, he is lured by another organisation 'B' with higher salary and better service conditions. After joining the new organisation, he will find that the workers are aggressive in their approach and the Management of the Company is too retrograde. The Manager is not given a free hand in negotiations. The employer wants large scale retrenchment of staff and workers to be effected with the motive to increase the profit. He is reluctant to give a fair deal to the workers with regard to salary, bonus, perks and other facilities to create congenial working conditions. Under such circumstances a workers' strike may take place. Depending on the attitudes of the parties, the situation may go out of hand also. Although the Personnel Manager alone is not responsible for all this, he might end up with being branded as 'in-efficient' and 'in-effective'.

Similarly, a Finance Manager earns a reputation when the various departments in the organisation contribute well in production, marketing, personnel Management etc. He may prove to be in-effective in spite of his knowledge, ability and hard work, if the production rate is consistently subnormal or the stocks pile up due to poor marketing strategy and therefore funds are always in short supply.

This reasoning applies with equal relevance to almost all the fields where Managers are required to manage. The other factors that could affect a Manager's efficiency are the team of the personnel working under him and the person whom he has to report to. By and large, the persons working under him can be moulded into a team, if the Manager is tactful and impartial and would make them realise that he would appreciate overall departmental efficiency rather than individuals' show off with their own performance. He should treat all the staff with due regard, according to their position and seniority and also develop a sort of personal rapport with every one of them. He should try to understand their problems in the work and either guide them or arrange to provide guidance to them. From time to time, he should hold meetings of the staff to discuss with them the goals and objectives of the organisation, specific targets of achievement/performance for the department. As far as possible, the allocation of the work should be done taking into consideration the aptitude and experience of each person. This part of the work is generally far simpler for any Manager with reasonable talents, although in certain cases, it involves tough and unpopular measures like dispensing with a chronically lazy or inefficient person or taking a firm stand with the personnel department or top management to prevent nepotism to get the better of fair play while selecting a candidate for a job in his department.

Quite often, a Manager finds that dealing with the person (let us call him 'top man') he reports to is not as easy as dealing with those working under him. If the 'top man' is reasonable and gives a free hand to the Manager within reasonable limits and understands his problems and appreciates his performance/achievements as what is practicable under given circumstances, the Manager can feel well satisfied.

But the 'top men' in some organisations are at times temperamental, greedy, having scant respect for the rules of the game or blind followers of a strict code of discipline. If a 'top man' is temperamental the Manager's fate depends on his moods. If he is greedy, the Manager can never satisfy him with any level of his and his department's performance. If he has got no respect for the rules of the game, the Manager will be required to adopt any dubious means for achieving the goal set before him. If he is too much of a disciplinarian, the Manager has to do a lot of tight rope walking. In such cases, the Manager will have little opportunity to show his talents and to achieve tangible results by being pragmatic and using his discretion where it is called for. A Manager will get a frustrating feeling, if he is taken to task for taking a decision under extraordinary conditions, on the plea that he has not consulted the 'top man' before-hand as per the code of discipline, although it is proved by the Manager that there was no time for such consultation and that the decision was actually very beneficial to the organisation.

Fortunately, not all the people to whom the Managers are required to report are of this type. Such Managers are the lucky ones who would be able to display their talents in full measure.

2

Managers and Their Negotiating Skills

Negotiating skills are very essential for Managers. Many times, in their careers, they are required to negotiate with individuals/groups/Unions/joint venture partners etc to arrive at settlements/agreements on a variety of subjects ranging from delicate labour disputes to mammoth business deals.

If the Managers are efficient and tactful, almost any problem could be solved by nipping it in the bud. Many of the strikes, lockouts, work to rule agitations could be averted. For doing this the Managers should be alert and sincere. They should keep their eyes and ears open to keep a watch on a situation as it develops. In their efforts to keep the situation under control and to find a solution to the problem, they should be responsive and understanding.

It may be surprising to note that some of the strikes and agitations have taken place for simple and flimsy reasons like an altercation between a worker and a supervisor or a delay in serving food and snacks in the canteen. Of course, some other strikes had to be resorted to because of genuine grievances and for the solution of long pending substantive issues.

If the Managers are imaginative and in constant touch with the concerned people, they could easily sort out the minor issues there and then, as soon as they crop up. The bigger issues too could be foreseen in many cases and negotiations set in motion well in time. Such an action would minimise the chances of the problems getting aggravated. Lack of responsiveness or total rejection from the Management side could make the other party to harden its stand. In due course, the issues will become prestige points.

Managers should remember that a 'give and take' attitude and 'fair play' are necessary for any negotiation to be successful. Taking advantage of the weakness of a party would amount to exploitation. A settlement reached in this way would not last long, as the aggrieved party would try to settle the scores at the earliest next opportunity. Similarly, conceding every demand of a party whether it is justified or not means surrender and capitulation. Although, this might have been done with good intentions, the other party may feel encouraged to come out with fresh demands. A negotiation could be considered as successful when all the parties feel more or less satisfied with the outcome and results in trouble-free and smooth functioning for a fairly long period. The timing of negotiation and right attitudes of the negotiations are very important for achieving satisfactory results.

Generally, the employers under-estimate the strength of the agitating employees. They think that by prolonging a strike, they could bring the employees to their "senses". Some others believe that they could arrive at an agreement favourable to themselves by striking a clandestine deal with the leaders of the employees' Union. Managers should do their best to remove such ideas from the minds of the employers. For, such agreements would not last long.

It should be appreciated that in quite a few cases, there are fairly good reasons for the employees to threaten to go on strike. Very often, these reasons pertain to their emoluments, perks and working conditions. If the Managers take timely action in persuading the employers to concede the demands to a reasonable extent, the workers' representatives too would find it easy to persuade the workers to withdraw their notice to strike.

But unfortunately, the trend has been to adopt a tough stand initially until the situation takes a serious turn and a crisis is created. Negotiations are then held in a highly surcharged atmosphere. After each meeting, both the sides issue statements accusing each other for the failure of the talks. The real reasons for the failure are the lack of mutual trust and the desire of each party to get the lion's share of the benefits to itself. After a number of such abortive meetings and prolonging the stalemate/strike/agitation for several weeks more, the parties would finally sign an agreement.

During that period, the public is put to great inconvenience. The agitating employees and their families would experience untold suffering. More often than not, such agitations take a violent turn causing loss of life and destruction of property. The loss of man-hours in each agitation is accounting for loss of production worth several crores of Rupees. If the Managers could persuade the employers to arrive at an amicable settlement before the deadline for strike, the employees could perhaps be satisfied with an offer amounting to much less than what the loss could be from a strike.

We could take the example of the recent work-to-rule agitation of the Engineering staff of Indian Airlines. Several flights had to be cancelled by Indian Airlines without notice, on account of this agitation. This author was one of the many passengers stranded at Goa due to a last minute cancellation of the flight from Goa to Delhi on the 16th of May. The plight of the passengers, particularly those who had to catch another flight at Delhi and/or to attend important meetings was really miserable. After waiting for several hours, we were taken to Bombay with an assurance that our seats were reserved by the flight IC 183 at 8.30 P.M. for Delhi. But at 8.00 P.M. we were told that the flight from Bombay to Delhi was also cancelled. For well over two hours, the officials of Indian Airlines did not know what to do. To the chagrin of the passengers, one official told that he would arrange for refund so that they could buy tickets from any other Airlines. It would have been appreciated if he had offered to arrange to book the stranded passengers on the flights of the other Airlines operators through his good offices. The loss incurred by the Indian Airlines due to this agitation was quite enormous.

In the same way, depending on where the strike takes place, the public in general and the customers in particular suffer considerably. The loss of production and workers' hardship too are quite tremendous.

Managers should remember the saying "A stitch in time saves nine". They should act promptly and decisively to prevent wasteful strikes, lock-outs, Bundhs, work-to-rule agitations etc. If they are frank and hold the talks in a cordial atmosphere, they could be fairly certain about achieving the above objective. Let their motto be 'avert a strike to keep the pace of development uninterrupted.'

3

Managers and Public Relations

Managers should not think that image building exercise is meant for politicians only. It is indeed required for Managers also, although to a lesser extent and in a different fashion. Maintenance of public relations should be given due importance for this purpose. Those who neglect this would have to regret for it at some stage in their careers. This could even result in their being branded as "egoistic", "arrogant", "unhelpful", "inefficient", "tactless" etc.

It is an admitted fact that many Managers have onerous responsibilities to discharge. Some times, the pressure of work is so great that some of them make it a habit to carry files and/or problems to their homes. Thereby, they deprive themselves of the much needed relaxation at home also. As a result, in due course, their faces will assume a tense and grim visage. Such an appearance usually tends to build an invisible barrier between them and the people they have to interact with.

Some of the causes that could drive the Managers to land up in such an undesirable situation are stated below.

(1) The pile of papers to be disposed of and the list of engagements to be fulfilled in a day could be mind boggling.

(2) Some chronic problems might be defying an early solution.

(3) The pressure from above (their bosses) for quick and satisfactory results could be nerve-wracking.

(4) The attitude and at times ineptitude of colleagues and subordinate staff and workers could be exasperating.

(5) The demands and expectations of the customers and the public may be too exacting to satisfy them.

Under these or similar conditions, managers should work out a clear-cut plan of action and a time-table for doing their work. They should remember the saying, "do not bite more than what you can chew" and take up only that much work which they can handle reasonably within the office timings. Taking into account the relative importance of the papers and/ or work, a portion of the same should be allocated to others. Delegation of duties with commensurate power to the right kind of people is the proper way to tackle this problem.

For chronic problems, they should examine whether the expertise from outside the organisation could be availed of for finding the correct solution. There are so many consultancy services in various specialised fields that it should not be difficult to adopt this course when plagued by intricate problems. Some Managers think that it reflects adversely on their abilities if they give such a suggestion to their superiors. But it is not really so. By wasting valuable time in a futile quest for solutions which are beyond their capacity to find, they would ultimately attract much more criticism for themselves.

The best way to tackle the pressure from above is to be frank and to tell the superiors what is possible to achieve and what are the resources required for achieving it. Many Managers make the mistake of trying to please their superiors temporarily or to buy time for themselves by painting too optimistic a picture. Such Managers will, in due course, find themselves in an awkward position giving explanations for their projections to have gone wrong.

At times, Managers would notice that some of their

colleagues and subordinate staff are not as co-operative and responsive as they expect them to be. A few of them could be even negligent or careless in their work also. A Manager has to judge the attitude of these people and tackle them tactfully in a manner that would not affect the overall efficiency. For instance, an important work should not be entrusted to a person known to be careless or inefficient. If a work is entrusted to a person who is prone to commit mistakes, it should be ensured that it is checked by some one else at an appropriate time. For changing the attitudes of colleagues, conciliatory methods would have a better chance to succeed than retaliatory methods.

For any organisation, the good-will and confidence of its customers and the public are very important for its success. Under no circumstances should any action be taken or words spoken that could antagonise them in any way. Supposing the price of a popular product has to be increased for compelling reasons, the same should be given due publicity to make the customers understand that there was no alternative left to the organisation. If there are complaints about the quality of a product or service, however much a Manager may feel the unreasonableness of the same, he should never brush them aside with a peremptory reply. He should look into the complaints and send individual replies to the complainants giving the particulars of the action taken on the complaints and the findings of the investigations within a reasonable time. Such an action would give a unique satisfaction to the customers. In due course, the number of complaints will come down. With regard to the complaints from the public about problems like pollution caused by an industry etc; a Manager must try to convince his superiors that the complaints of the public should be attended to, at least in stages. The public should be given the impression that the organisation is not ignoring their interests. This can be done by undertaking some welfare measures for their benefit, in right earnest. If the demands of the public go beyond a reasonable limit, the help of the local leaders must be enlisted for keeping them under check.

Under pressure of work, some Managers lose their patience. They tend to become irritable and easily excited. They prefer to remain aloof and in-communicado. Such Managers may end up being branded as "failures" despite their knowledge, hard work and sincerity. Therefore it is very essential that Managers keep their "cool" while talking to others. It would be better for their image if they "listen more and speak less". They should say even an unpleasant thing in a polite manner.

They should plan their time table in such a fashion that they are available to meet people at all reasonable times in a day. The personal secretaries of some Managers always seem to tell any callers that they are busy in meetings. Some people coming from long distances to meet a Manager would feel utterly disappointed with such replies. The secretary should at least give an appointment at some other time on the same day or the next day. If possible, the Secretary should talk with the callers and ascertain the purpose of their visit and give the particulars needed by them, if they are readily available. If a Manager avoids meeting people and is curt while talking with colleagues and subordinate staff he would lose his image very badly.

Therefore, any Manager who wants to be successful in his career should cultivate certain qualities like "being calm and cheerful", "being polite and patient", "being friendly and helpful" and being "appreciative and understanding" right from the beginning of his career. He should also give due importance to his dress and appearance as they would create the first impression of any person. He should set apart a little time daily to meet people and make them feel that he is easily accessible. He should never fail to attend social functions to which he has been invited. He should mingle freely with the guests giving the impression that he is enjoying himself in their company.

In these days when informality is encouraged, it is not advisable for Managers to sit in their ivory towers concentrating on the work only. No doubt, a Manager has to be proficient in his field and should possess leadership qualities. But in addition, he has to maintain good public relations and build a good image of himself for ensuring alround success in his career.

4

Recruitment Policies – Some Vital Aspects

In any organisation, the management has to give due importance to its recruitment policy and the fixing of salary and perks to the workers, staff and officers. Whatever be the nature of its business and the extent of the mechanisation, no organisation can run the show without manpower. In fact, in our country the dependence on man power is larger than in many other countries, even after the scientific and technological advances made in the recent past. If the persons recruited for doing the various jobs prove to be like the proverbial square peg in a round hole, the organisation would not be able to survive.

Almost all the organisations seem to have adopted policies and norms in this regard, rather mechanically. Very few are applying their minds to formulate a policy suited to their own needs. As a result, the processes of recruitment and retrenchment are repeated alternately, all too often. If a proper policy is formulated and implemented in right earnest, this costly and painful exercise can be curtailed to its bearest minimum.

In the last few years, several companies have witnessed a change in their managements as a sequel to their take-overs by other corporate groups. After each take over, almost invariably the management directs its attention to the possibility of reduction in the strength of the staff, workers and officers. The result is that the officers, staff and workers will spend sleepless nights brooding over what could happen to their jobs.

No one can deny that stability and security of job are the prime requisites for happiness of any employee. If a Democle's sword hangs on his head every now and then, he would not only lose his peace of mind but also his efficiency and presence of mind.

Modern managements are appearing to be least concerned about these problems of their employees. In the name of the so-called "competitiveness" in "the market oriented economy", they are adopting any conceivable methods for achieving higher productivity and profitability. They would not care even if some of these methods are not ethical. Their only obsession is to achieve their objective. Some of the employees would have rendered a yeomen service to their organisations for several years, in the past. One could very well imagine as to how they would feel or what would their fate be, if they are asked to quit on one fine day under a scheme like "voluntary retirement scheme". The managements would not have given anything extra to their staff, workers and officers for the profits and benefits derived by the organisations due to their special efforts in the past. Then, what justification could be there for removing them from service in this manner? Some of the reasons given by the management for such an action are as follows.

(1) The strength of the workers and staff is found to be in excess of the optimum requirement as per a study conducted by a management consultant.

(2) There is not enough work for a few people as the assignments entrusted to them are nearing completion.

(3) Updating of technology or modernisation of the plant or closing down of a division has rendered some of the officers, staff and workers surplus.

While taking this kind of action, the managements are trying to ape the management styles in America and Europe blindly without noticing the difference in their working conditions, social back grounds and culture. In those countries the salary structure is such that the staff and workers can save enough for facing the eventuality of remaining unemployed for some time. They have also got far better employment opportunities. Therefore they could get an alternative employment within a reasonable time. They are also covered by insurance/social security scheme etc. In our country, the salaries being low, the savings of these employees are negligible. Getting an alternative job is too difficult due to poor employment opportunities. There are no insurance and social security schemes in our country to enable the retrenched employees to get some stipend during the period of their unemployment.

Indian tradition and culture call for the employees' interests to be taken care of even when the employers are passing through critical times. But, in the recent past, these values have been given the go-bye. A man is treated well as long as he is useful and he is dropped like a hot potato, the moment it is realised that there is no further use of that man or somebody else could be a little more useful in his place.

If a society has to be happy, the values of humanity should take precedence over the inanimate commercial values. If the choice is between making a profit of 40 per cent by retrenching a couple of hundred employees and remaining content with a profit of 30 per cent by keeping those employees also on the rolls, a management which cares for ethics and values of humanity must opt for the latter. It is not suggested here that retrenchment on the grounds of inefficiency and indiscipline should not be resorted to. In the extreme case when the very survival of the organisation is at stake unless retrenchment of some employees is effected, such an action could be understood and condoned.

Although before an election all the political parties promise to increase the employment opportunities by creating more jobs, Governments formed by these parties are doing pretty little in this regard. What is even worse, they are abolishing several posts at various levels in the Government departments and public sector organisations. They are turning a blind eye to the massive retrenchment schemes launched by many companies in the private sector.

Some companies recruit personnel without correctly estimating their needs. When they get good profits and have some ambitious plans for expansion/diversification, they recruit some more personnel indiscriminately without ascertaining whether they would be rendered surplus in due course.

About 25 years ago, for any senior position, a minimum of 15 to 20 years experience was being prescribed for the candidates besides the requisite academic qualification. But in the last 10 years, the trend has changed drastically. Even for top posts in many private sector companies, persons with hardly 5 years experience are being preferred. Does it mean that the persons of younger age group only could perform the functions of the top brass better than persons in the older age group? Does it mean that a long experience of a person is no longer needed for posts in higher echelons?

The gap between the salaries and perks of the top level Managers and those of the officers, staff and workers is widening day-by-day. Many high salaried people keep flitting from one post to another at least in the first few years of their service as and when they get a post with higher sarlary and perks. Loyalty to an organisation and commitment to the accomplishment of a job are becoming very rare to find. These unhealthy trends are the natural off-shoots of the haphazard recruitment policies.

A few suggestions are given below which could be helpful in correcting these unhealthy trends.

(1) Ascertain the requirement and estimate the number of persons to be recruited in different grades.

(2) While calling for candidates, specify the job requirement and a general minimum academic qualification instead of laying down rigid limits on age and qualification and experience in a specific field.

(3) Keep a list of the candidates who could not be selected but are good enough for the advertised posts. If a selected candidate leaves the job or the post falls vacant for any other reason within a few months after the recruitment, the organisation should correspond with the candidates on their list and select one of them instead of calling for fresh applications.

(4) Wooing the staff of one organisation by another by direct contact is not a healthy practice. This should be discouraged.

(5) The staff and workers should be stabilised and given a feeling that their posts are secure except under extra ordinary circumstances.

(6) Train the new recruits in their respective jobs. This is very important to ensure efficiency and desired output.

(7) The salaries and perks should be reasonable for all grades depending on the nature of their jobs. The gap in the salaries between any two consecutive grades should not be too large.

(8) Before recruitment of new personnel, think well whether they are really required and they could be maintained on the rolls at least for 10 years.

(9) Retrenchment of staff and workers should be resorted to only in the worst crisis threatening the very existence of the organisation. Otherwise this course should not be adopted except in rare cases of in-efficiency and indiscipline.

(10) Last but not the least, candidates hailing from around the place of work should be given preference for appointment, when they have more or less equal qualification with other candidates coming from long distances. This policy has many advantages for the employer and the employees. The employees would not like to change their jobs in such a case. They would take less time to visit their native place in case of emergencies.

5

Role of Managers in Economic and Industrial Development

The pace and extent of economic and industrial development largely depend on the degree of the skills and application of the Managers. Once, a plan for a development project is formulated and the funds are granted for its implementation, Managers in the various departments are required to play a positive role for achieving the desired goal.

We all know that often such projects are getting abnormally delayed resulting in heavy over-run on their cost. Some of the causes for the delay and cost over-run are (a) faulty planning, (b) inadequate preparatory work (c) cumbersome rules (d) corruption and (e) Court cases. For hastening the development process, the Managers should be given more powers coupled with higher responsibility.

Let us elaborate each of the above mentioned points.

(a) *Faulty planning*: A multi-crore water supply project was taken up without ascertaining the availability of sufficient quantity of water at the source. Another huge industrial project with a foreign collaboration was starred without making sure that there was enough demand for its end product. A major canal project was hastily taken up without acquiring nearly 70% of the land required for its construction. A large housing scheme was taken up at a remote place where there was no hope of getting the infra structural facilities like protected water supply, drainage, electric power, public transport, market etc.

Of course, it is needless to say that all these projects are either abandoned or progressing at a snail's speed. The examples given are only a few, but there are many development schemes like these which had to be given up altogther or suspended for long durations, after large sums of money having been spent on them. It is, therefore, essential that while planning a development project, all aspects of the project including its viability are thoroughly examined.

(b) *Inadequate preparatory work*: A lot of preparatory work has to be done before the actual commencement of a project.

Let us take a construction project as an example. The preparatory work in this case includes appointment of the required staff, getting ready as many detailed drawings of the project as possible, if not all the drawings, procurement of materials like cement and steel in sufficient quantities, fixing the right kind of contractors/suppliers for the construction and allied works, arrangements for elec. power, water approach roads, office and transport facilities. Programmes of many projects have gone haywire because of lack of preparatory work before launching upon them.

(c) *Cumbersome rules*: In the work order for the construction of a building, there was an item for the supply and fixing of steel windows including glazing and painting. The contractor had procured the windows and fixed them in position. However, glazing and painting were deferred till the completion of plastering of walls which was expected to take a couple of months more. The contractor claimed payment at 75% of the rate for this item and the Manager in charge of the construction had recommended it. But the accounts Dept. pointed out that there was no provision in the work order for making payment at a part rate. This and some similar things had resulted in a cash flow problem and delay in the work.

In another project, the quantity of RCC work actually carried out had exceeded the quantity shown in the work order. The payment for this extra quantity could not be released until it was approved by the President of the Company whose office was located 400 km away from the project site.

In the Govt. Departments payments are delayed in April and May as money will not be available until fresh allotment has been made for a financial year starting on the 1st of April. This allotment is generally delayed by 6 to 8 weeks. The unspent money out of the allotment for the previous financial year lapses at the end of March. Why can't the rules be changed to ensure the availability of sufficient fund in April also every year, by allowing a carry-over from the previous year or by making fresh allotment in March itself for the next financial year? For fear of the funds getting lapsed by the end of March, some departments are resorting to heavy purchases of cement and similar materials even though they are not required for several months thereafter. Materials like cement are getting damaged because of long storage, thereby causing heavy loss.

One project took a little longer time than the stipulated time for its completion. The agreement provided for quarterly payment towards compensation on account of escalation of prices based on the whole-sale prices index. The Govt. department had delayed granting of extension of time because of their long winding procedure. Meanwhile the officials asked the contractor to continue with the work. But they refused to pay the "escalation" bill saying that the agreement did not provide for such payment until the extension of time was granted.

(d) *Corruption*: This is perhaps the single most important cause for the delays in the economic and industrial development of our country. A common man thinks of corruption as a ticket collector extracting a few rupees more than the normal charges from the passenger for alloting a sleeper berth in a train or similar things in a number of offices like Municipal office, R.T.O.'s office or a Taluq office. No doubt, such cases of corruption are bad and have to be condemned. But what he does not know so well is the macro scale corruption which is so rampant where disbursement of large sums of money is involved and is ruining the economy and retarding the developmental process inexorably.

It is common knowledge that whenever a contractor's bill is passed and payment made, the contractor pays a fixed percentage to all the concerned officials in many of the Government Departments. When an order for a large consignment of machinery is placed, the supplier usually gives a fixed lumpsum amount or a certain percentage of the value of the order to the officials who have processed, recommended and signed the order. More than these corrupt and despisable officials, the contractors, suppliers and the business people are getting away with chunks of money undeservedly with the help and connivance of these officials.

A large portion of the amounts received in the form of mobilisation advance, machinery advance, term loans given by Banks and financial institutions are diverted into their personal coffers by some of the owners/promoters/heads of these organisations. At a later date, they also come out with fictitious/or inflated claims and revised rates etc. The corrupt officials help and guide them in securing huge chunks of money from the amount meant for the implementation of the projects. Ultimately, perhaps only about 70% of the money allocated for a project is spent for the intended purpose. The cost of escalation of the project accounts for another 30% to 50% on an average on account of delays in its implementation.

Thus if the corruption is rooted out the pace of development would be much faster and the benefits would almost double for the same investment.

(e) *Court cases*: In a democracy, courts have an important role to play. They are expected to ensure that every citizen enjoys the rights enshrined in our constitution.

But, unfortunately many individuals/organisations/ business houses are misusing the courts taking advantage of certain provisions in law for stalling developmental projects or for getting large sums of money as compensation etc. from the amount meant for such projects. While it is laudable that the courts are available for individuals/organisations to approach for protecting their rights, it is regrettable that these individuals/organisations are succeeding so often in stalling the development work and or garnering large chunks of money for themselves. Some steps should be taken to check this kind of happenings in a suitable manner which should be evolved after eliciting the views of the people in all walks of life.

Managers should be able to tackle the problems mentioned above in an effective manner. They should take responsibility for delivering the goods in their respective areas and should make it clear to their reporting officers that they should be given commensurate discretionery powers. At a time when people think that ethics are given the go-bye in most of the business and government offices, Managers on whom the Nation sets a great store as the new breed of trained go-getters and high-tech executives should come forward with their own blemishless conduct to reestablish the ethical values in our daily lives and to give an impetus to the economic and industrial development.

6

Some Managers and their Perverse Fixations

A post of a Manager is usually an important one. A Manager is vested with powers/responsibility to lead a team of workers/staff in an organisation. At a senior level, a Manager is expected to be in charge of a Department or a Division or an organisation depending on its size and volume of operations/activities. A Manager's attitude, temparament and style of functioning would have a marked influence and impact on the work-culture of the team of workers/staff he/she is in charge of. As is common with most of the human beings, some Managers too have certain oddities in their nature and they show up in their styles of functioning. Bearing in mind the likely ill-effects that could be produced by such oddities on the psychology and work-culture of the workers/staff, those Managers should make a conscious effort to curb their urge to act on the basis of certain unfounded notions and personal fads. Perhaps, a few examples given below would make this point clearer.

One Manager's favourite saying was that if "overtime work" was allowed, workers would not work during the normal working hours. He used to repeat this very often before his staff. Therefore, the staff used to be mortally afraid of engaging workers on "overtime" even in an emergency situation. It may be true that in order to earn a little extra wages (usually, double wages are paid for over time work), some workers may be on the look-out for some overtime work. But it is an out-right exaggeration to say that once an "overtime work" is permitted, the workers would not work at all, in the normal working hours. Actually, what is required to be done is to keep a control on the "overtime work" by (1) trying to complete the works in the normal working hours as far as possible by deploying/planning the optimum work force and (2) by limiting the "overtime work" for each worker to a specified number of hours within a week or a month.

A Manager's strictness with regard to "overtime work" could be wrought with consequences like loss of production in a factory or delay in disposal of some urgent papers/matters in an office. The cost on account of the loss of production and delay in disposal of urgent papers/matters could be far higher than the cost of "overtime wages".

Another Manager in a factory had the habit of saying that "he loved the production Department and considered the maintenance Department as a necessary evil". These words had produced a sense of complacency in the minds of the production staff and a feeling of dejection in the minds of the maintenance staff. The Manager had obviously failed to appreciate the complementary nature of the roles of the two Departments. Unless the maintenance Department ensures that the machinery is kept in good working condition, the production staff cannot achieve their production targets. The Manager's words are like a football player saying that he loves his right leg and he is not bothered about his left leg. The reason is that he plays foot-ball with his right leg. But, he should realise that unless both of his legs are in tact and act in unision, he would not be able to play the game effectively.

Yet another Manager would like to evaluate figures about production or wages or cost of materials or anything like that as a percentage of a base figure only. No doubt, this is an accepted practice in any business organisation or a factory or a Government Department. However, problems would arise if this method of evaluation is extended to absurd limits. For instance, a Supervisor in charge of a Garage wanted 20 meter long teflon pipe of 20 mm diameter for use in spray painting of the vehicles. Until then, polythene pipe was being used for this purpose. The Manager wanted to know their relative costs. The cost of teflon pipe was Rs300/- whereas the cost of polythene pipe was Rs100/- only. The Manager refused permission to purchase the teflon pipe as it was 200 per cent costlier than the polythene pipe! He was not impressed even by the reason that teflon pipe is more durable. The Manager appeared to be unaware that where the total cost is trivial, the evaluation by the method of percentages is not so relevant and some times could give a totally misleading picture also.

Once, a political leader tried to impress his audience by saying that his party had improved its strength in the Lok Sabha by 100 per cent in the election that was held a little earlier. The actual fact was that the party in question had two seats in the Lok Sabha earlier and the number had gone upto four after the election! It should be borne in mind that even a small percentage like one or two of large figures running into crores of rupees is much more than a comparatively higher percentage like ten or twenty of smaller figures running into hundreds or thousands of rupees only. Therefore, while evaluating on the basis of percentages, one should not ignore the figures/values in their absolute terms also.

The next example is of a Manager whose first item on the agenda for improving profitability is always "reduction of the strength of staff and workers". There are many other factors like raw material cost, machinery maintenance cost, packaging and despatching cost, and the banking charges where one should give due attention as any small saving on them would be much more than the saving on account of reduction of staff and workers, as their wages constitute only a small fraction of the costs of the above items. Retrenchment of staff and workers would create a sense of insecurity and dissatisfaction among all the workers and staff. They would be demoralised and would be particularly disenchanted with the Manager initiating and/or implementing the scheme. A wise Manager should think of other ways like those mentioned below for improving profitability.

(1) Ensure that the raw material is of good quality and it is purchased at competitive price.

(2) Reduce the plant shut-down time by ensuring good maintenance of the machinery and using quality spare parts.

(3) Maintain good relations between Management and workers in order to avoid loss of production on account of strikes, lock-outs etc. Also enforce safety rules to avoid accidents that could result in loss to the concerned persons and expenses to the management.

(4) Update the technology. Improve the production by giving incentives to workers for giving more than normal out-put consistently for a month at a stretch.

(5) Minimise wastage of materials, in the form of deterioration, spillage etc and loss due to pilferage in stores or in transport.

(6) Ensure that the items manufactured are of the required quality and the rejection rate is as low as possible.

(7) Proper planning with regard to borrowings from the Banks and payment of taxes, and last but not the least,

(8) Ensure that money is not siphoned out by the people in the form of commissions and bribes.

Only after the above points are exhausted should a Manager think of retrenchment as the last resort if it is absolutely necessary to save an organisation from bankruptcy or any such thing. Any organisation should think well before recruiting staff and workers, keeping their strength within the optimum limits. There are some instances of the work suffering heavily for want of sufficient manpower after the completion of an "operation retrenchment". The organisation had to recruit fresh staff and workers once again.

I will conclude this chapter by quoting one more example of a Manager who had secured the post more by luck and circumstances than by his record of service or abilities. He was like a "doubting Thomas" and was suspicious of every body's actions. He was afraid of taking any decision lest he should be held responsible for anything going wrong. He got this post in a factory of a core industry in the private sector when the factory construction and installation of machinery were in their final stages. It was a crucial period just before the production was due to commence. Whenever somebody was going to him for a decision, he used to appoint a committee of two or three officers to go into the matter. Everyone knows how the committees work. The resulting delays used to be abnormal.

Fortunately, a majority of Managers seem to be rational, systematic and free from the kind of the oddities, fixations and vacillations described above. But how much better it would be if the rest of the Managers too could emulate them, by correcting themselves after a little introspection?

7

Top Managers and Decision Making

It is universally acknowledged that one person cannot be proficient in every field of activity in a large organisation. Depending on one's qualification, aptitude and experience, the person could become knowledgeable and efficient in one or, at the most, a few departments only. If anyone claims knowledge of every-thing about every department, he must be living in a fool's paradise. If such a person starts meddling with works that are expected to be done by others possessing specific expertise, the end-result could be quite disastrous.

The persons in top management should be content with laying down guidelines to the managers working under them and reviewing their performance, periodically. They could take corrective steps whenever they think that the things are going astray. But they should never take upon themselves the burden of the duties of a Manager of a department with which they are not conversant. A few top Managers are too egoistic to admit that tackling certain problems all by themselves is beyond their capacity as they do not possess the required specific knowledge and expertise. Such persons complicate the problems by making a vain bid at solving them, ignoring the Managers meant to do that work.

Some top Managers by virtue of their high position tend to

thrust their decisions on the departments without even listening to the viewpoints of the concerned Managers. It is not ruled out that now and then, such decisions taken on a hunch may prove to be correct, although the decision-making process is irrational. But it is more likely that such decisions will prove to be incorrect and even detrimental to the interests of the organisation. At times, the over-enthusiasm of a top Manager and the actions emanating therefrom could prove to be very costly to the organisation.

These points could be illustrated better by stating how a company suffered a huge financial loss and a slur on its reputation as a result of an irrational and hasty decision taken by its top Manager, although his intentions were good. The company in question had decided to close one of its divisions. Although, the process was set in motion towards this end, the operations of the division were still continuing, as the contracts taken up earlier remained incomplete.

The top Manager of the company was too eager to dispense with the services of the employees in that division as a step towards the set objective. One fine day, he took a snap decision to entrust the task of completing the unfinished contract work to an agency on what he thought was a "back to back basis." This person had no experience in this kind of contract works, although he had earned a reputation for efficiency in another division devoted to manufacturing and sales work, before his promotion to the top post.

He thought that the Agency fixed by him would successfully fulfil the company's contractual obligations in the construction project, without any need for the company's staff to supervise at the site. He had believed the words of the Agency without checking with the executives of the division which was in the process of being wound up. He believed that by doing so, he was saving for the company the expenditure on the salaries of the staff at the work site and also hastening the winding up process. He also thought that as the Agency seemed to agree to work on a back to back basis, the company would not lose monetarily, apart from a portion of the expected profit.

In the beginning, the management of the company appreciated the "wisdom" and "dynamism" of the top Manager. But it did not take long before the true colours of the Agency were revealed. The Agency interpreted the brief work order given to it in a totally unexpected manner. It had claimed payment for much larger quantity of work than the quantity that the company could claim form its client. The Agency claimed for the quantity arrived at by its own measurements. They could not be verified as the company's staff was withdrawn.

Tongues started wagging, expressing doubts about the integrity of the top Manager when the people came to know about the more-than-generous terms on which the Agency was entrusted with the work. Very soon, it became evident that the Agency's greed for making unreasonable profit at the expense of the company was insatiable. The company was required to pump in money, whereas it could have earned a handsome profit with its attractive rates, had the work been carried out in the usual manner, with its staff posted at site to supervise the work.

Another company had indeed earned a good profit in doing a similar work for the same client, by getting its work supervised by its own staff. But, the company which tried to save an expenditure of Rs 5 lakhs to Rs 6 lakhs on the salaries of its staff at site for a period of one year was deprived of its profit to the tune of Rs 25 lakhs in that period. At such a late stage, the top Manager had realised that his decision had proved to be "penny wise and pound foolish".

Meanwhile, the attitude of the Agency was becoming more and more unreasonable, day by day. The client's complaints about the unsatisfactory quality and progress of the work increased in frequency and severity. The company found itself in an unenviable position, with its reputation at stake. The top manager was embarrassed at the turn of the events in this fashion. When the situation appeared to be quite serious, and going out of hand, he called the executives conversant with the contract works and asked them to salvage the company from the mess.

It was only by a quirk of circumstances and a foolish move made by the Agency that the company could get rid of the Agency, finally. The Agency agreed to withdraw, hoping that it could squeeze out of the company another Rs 50 lakhs or so by interpreting the conditions of the work order in its favour, without taking the trouble of doing the balance work. The company had then posted its own staff for supervising and completing the balance work as per its contract.

Had the top Manager asked the concerned executives to give a report on the pros and cons of the decision he intended to take, the company would have been saved from this unsavoury experience. Indeed, it could have earned a profit of well over Rs 30 lakhs even after accounting for the salary of the staff, which the top Manager tried to save for the company.

The lesson from this for the students of Management studies as well as practising Managers is that they should believe in the saying that "haste makes waste". It is not suggested that the Managers should be slow in taking decisions or in implementing them. But, surely, they should act only after going through the reports or listening to the advice of those who are supposed to have the knowledge and expertise in the relevant subject. If they do not want to subscribe to the wisdom of the saying "slow and steady wins the race", in the present jet age, they should, at least, not forget the word "caution" while treading on an uncharted course.

8

Human Relations in Industry

Generally, the prosperity of a country is dependent on its industrial growth. Of course, there are a few countries which have become prosperous because of their natural resources like oil. Some other countries have achieved prosperity through trading and tourism. In our country, we are laying accent on industrial growth for this purpose like a vast majority of the developing countries.

The foremost aim of any industry is to achieve higher productivity. "Higher production at lower cost" is the pet slogan of all the industrial units. Productivity depends on several factors like the quality of the machines, technology adopted, type of raw materials, techniques of quality control and above all, the people at work. For every machine a man is required for its operation and maintenance.

Let us take the example of the cement industry. One may procure the latest type of excavators and haulers for working on a limestone quarry. But without men they cannot be operated. The performance and output of the machines are directly related to the efficiency as well as the physical and mental condition of their operators. Men are also required to locate the deposits of limestone and other raw materials. Similarly, man plays a key role at every stage of the manufacturing process like crushing limestone, correction of raw meal/slurry, production of clinker and grinding of clinker with gypsum. In addition to these jobs, men are also employed for carrying out other functions like management, planning, research and development, quality control, marketing, office correspondence and maintenance of accounts. All of them have to work with efficiency and in co-operation with one another if the goals of the industry have to be achieved. But, if a few of them are negligent in their duties and disinterested about the results and pull in different directions, it could produce an adverse effect on the overall performance of the industry. Therefore, it is imperative for the survival, viability and growth of an industry that all the people involved should do their work properly and display a team spirit and enthusiasm to reach the targets set for their industry. In this context, maintenance of good human relations assumes a great importance for inculcating in the minds of the people a commitment to work whole-heartedly and unitedly for achieving the common objective.

The main reasons for the deficiencies in the human effort are three-fold. The first is the lack of training. Unless a person is well trained and becomes skilled and competent, he will not be able to do his work efficiently. Therefore, the employees should be given proper training/briefing/induction at the appropriate stages. Merely blaming an employee for his inefficiency would not solve a problem. At times, it may be found that he is better suited for a job other than the one for which he has been appointed. If such a possibility is there, the person concerned should be transferred to the job which he can perform more efficiently.

The second reason is "ego" displayed by some people. By their behaviour, they try to give an impression to the others that they are superior and their work is more important and hence they should be respected and obeyed. Such attitude of these people could do considerable harm to the human relations. The aggrieved people would try to avoid meeting the egoistic persons and develop a hostile feeling for them gradually. Such a development is not good for any industry.

Therefore, an effort should be made to make the people shed their ego. It should be driven home to the minds of the people that all are playing their allotted roles, each one being complementary to the rest and not whole by itself. If some one has a higher academic qualification and is more experienced and talented, he may occupy a supervisory or managerial post with higher salary and perks. But, because of this, he should not think that he has got a right to treat the others in a shabby manner. It should be remembered that one harsh word from a supervisor may upset the spirits of a sincere worker. A superiority complex displayed by an officer may build an invisible barrier between him and his subordinates. There was a time when employees were expected to tolerate any kind of treatment. But now, in the changed social structure, dignity of individual has been recognised and has to be conceded.

This is possible only by creating a congenial atmosphere by organising as often as possible social and entertainment functions wherein people can come in intimate contact with one another. Such meetings outside the place of work would help them understand one another better and develop a feeling of camaraderie among themselves. A feeling that each one by doing his duty well is helping all others in accomplishing a goal would be fostered in everybody's mind.

The third reason is the employees' feeling that they are being given a raw deal by the management. It should be remembered that a man can give his best performance when he is free from worries and grievances. Discrimination in treatment, promotion etc based on considerations other than "performance" like caste, relationship, language, religion could leave a bitter feeling in the minds of the affected persons. Thoughtless remarks by and harsh behaviour of the management in the name of strictness and discipline could alienate the staff and workers. Suppose that the out-turn per worker is fixed on the basis of a work study conducted under ideal conditions on a few exceptionally good workers, an average worker will find it hard to achieve that out-turn. In his anxiety to achieve the target, he may have to over exert himself and in the process the quality of the product may be diluted. Over-exertion not only leads to health problems but also gives rise to animosity for the management. Finally, it is an admitted fact that all people work for earning their salaries and enjoying their perks. Suppose, the management is niggardly in fixing their salaries and perks in spite of good profits being made by the industry, the staff and workers would feel reluctant to co-operate with the management. Many of them would be on the look-out for an alternative job also. Such exploitation of the employees is being resorted to by a few employers/ managements by taking advantage of the present conditions of unemployment and under-employment.

For setting up an industry, the management might have arranged for the necessary finances, tapping the appropriate resources. But it is the employees, who are instrumental in transforming the plans of the management into a reality with their hard work, skill and knowledge. It is again their sincere working and devotion which are required for the efficient running of the industry and for ensuring reasonable profits. In view of this, it is advisable in the interest of the parties concerned, that the management should give the employees a feeling of being its partners. If this is done wholeheartedly, many of the strikes, lock-outs and consequent loss of production could be avoided.

It should be understood that a constant effort is needed for building proper human relations and maintaining them in a harmonious manner. The labour welfare and human resources development departments have a special responsibility in achieving this objective, although other departments and the individual employees also have to make their own contribution. Unfortunately, in many industries, the labour welfare and HRD departments are acting as though they are there to merely carry out the wishes of the management. There are instances of the officials of these departments creating divisions and differences between the employees for gaining an advantage in negotiations with their representatives. By driving a wedge between them, they try to keep the different groups at the mercy of the management.

Similarly the workers' Unions are often adopting rigid postures thinking that their duty lies in always opposing the actions of the management. In some industrial units, there are too many unions and they pull in different directions. This is resulting in weakening the cause of the workers. The attitudes of the labour welfare and HRD Departments and the workers' unions should undergo a change for the better, if the problems related to human element have to be reduced in the industries. Perhaps the following suggestions could be followed for achieving the above objective.

(1) Avoid taking inflexible attitudes in meetings for resolving disputes.

(2) Laws and rules should not be considered as instruments to keep the employees under perpetual threat. They should be used to punish in rare cases of wilful negligence and/or proven in-efficiency only.

(3) It should be realised that people would not normally fail to respond to friendliness, affection and acts of kindness. Suppose a supervisor expresses sympathy for the illness of a near and dear relation of a worker, it would surely touch the heart of the concerned worker. A friendly chat of an officer with his subordinate would enhance the subordinate's regard for him. A benevolent gesture of a management in letting an employee go with a warning when a sterner punishment like a suspension could have been justified according to the strict letter of the law could warm the hearts of the employees for the management.

(4) The labour welfare and HRD departments and the employees' union should be constructive in their attitudes. Their actions should not be aimed at harming each other's interests.

(5) Ensure greater transperancy in the working of the industry to remove the suspicion of the employees that they are given a raw deal. Management should be liberal in the sharing of the profits with the employees by offering reasonable bonus etc.

(6) Keep the representatives of the employees informed on important matters pertaining to the running of the industry. The declaration of holidays, provision of amenities like housing, medical facilities, transport etc should be done after coming to an amicable understanding through mutual discussion.

(7) Organise training programmes for the employees from time to time. Encourage team spirit. Listen to suggestions wherever they may come from. Give token rewards for innovative suggestions and bright ideas.

(8) Provide facilities like club, playgrounds, parks and co-operative stores. A fund should be created to help the needy by giving loans at nominal interest.

(9) Arrange picnics and other entertainment programmes like cinema, dance etc periodically. If the industry is very large, these arrangements could be made departmentwise.

(10) Avoid vindictiveness. Encourage participation and healthy inter-action of the people in parties and gatherings.

(11) Introduce welfare schemes for the families of employees. Take note of the success of their children in exams etc and give the employees a feeling that the management has at its heart the welfare and well-being of its employees and their families.

(12) Settle the accounts of those who have retired or resigned or have been retrenched without delay and in an equitable manner.

(13) Let the employees feel that they are wanted in the industry. This will help in reducing the exodus of the employees.

(14) Take note of the talents and aptitudes of the employees and try to accommodate them in jobs in which they could feel at home.

(15) Keep a watch on the work load of the employees. At times some are overworked and some others have much lighter duties. To the extent possible reduce the burden of the overworked employees by reallocating some of their duties. Keep doing this exercise periodically.

(16) Ensure safety at work place. Expenditure on safety equipment should not be curtailed in the name of economy. Enforce all safety rules and follow safety precautions.

Indeed, this list is not complete, as there are many more items which could be added to it.

Counselling and correcting the attitudes of the people and taking sympathetic note of grievances of the people are required to be done on a regular basis for creating harmonious human relations. Once this is achieved, half the problems in the industry will have been solved. Human psychology being more intricate and complex than any machine, it is only proper that enough attention is devoted to understand and tackle it just as the maintenance of machines is attended to in a systematic manner.

9

Role of Marketing after Liberalisation of Industrial Policy

The importance of marketing in business organisatins can not be over emphasised. Marketing encompasses wide ranging activities like forecasting demand for a product, sales, after-sales service, ascertaining the changing needs of the customers for incorporating necessary changes in the product and educating the customers about the advantages of using their product. In a situation where a product is in short supply, the importance of marketing is generally not understood fully. However, if the market is flooded with a product of several brands, the role of marketing gets accentuated.

In our country, many of the items needed by the people ranging from food items, consumer goods to luxury goods like refrigerators and cars are in short supply. But very soon this scenario may change. There is a prospect of the sellers' market of today turning into a buyers' market, if the multinational companies get a firm foot hold as a result of the Govenment's liberalisation of the industrial and economic policies. The inflow of foreign capital too will hasten this process.

For reviewing the present situation, let us take a few examples like cement, steel, detergent, fertilizer, soaps, toothpaste, textiles etc. Production of most of these items is much lower than the demand. Hitherto, import of these and similar items is discouraged and restricted in order to give protection to the domestic industries/business. As a result, the customer is left with no option but to buy what is available in the market. Even a product which is not really good enough for a customer's liking is sold without much difficulty. Some of the businessmen give scant respect to the ordinary customers, despite their outward pretensions of sympathy and concern for their problems. The customer is often groaning under the conditions of scarcity resulting in high prices, poor quality and little after-sales service. At times, it is quite anamolous to find that a product of one brand considered to be inferior in quality to the same product of another brand is priced higher than the other. But still, it is also sold in the market. Where there is no control from the Government, the prices are increased every now and then as per the whims and fancies of the manufacturers/producers/businessmen. Where the controls are imposed, black marketing is resorted to.

Recently in my train journeys I came across some business people and I was stunned by their attitude and thinking about business, Government controls and customers. One of them who owns a rice mill told that hoarding of paddy and rice is often resorted to for increasing the market prices before releasing them for sale. Another businessmen dealing in leather goods advocated removal of all curbs on the business to usher in what he termed a "free market". He said that he failed to understand why anybody should be taken to task for having brought an item like a watch/VCR/camera from abroad and selling the same at a profit within the country. He wondered why any action should be taken against him as he has not committed a theft. Both these people were justifying hoarding and smuggling as right means for earning profits in business. I am sure that many business people have got the same attitude and out-look. Their main concern is to make as much profit for themselves as possible. The means for achieving this need not necessarily be clean and strictly in accordance with the law.

Suppose you buy a Mixie or a refrigerator and find some

defect in it after a few days. You should not be surprised if you are made to run from pillar to post before the defect is attended to by the manufacturer. Very often, even to get the attention of the dealer/manufacturer to your problem, you may have to make half a dozen phone calls and/or to visit the shop two or three times. Many customers find that the weights and measures of the items are less than what are shown on their labels. Generally speaking, the manufacturers/producers/dealers do not pay as much attention as required to the quality aspect of the product/items/goods/services.

Once the market conditions change and the 'customer satisfaction' would become the key factor for the survival of a business, marketing work will assume its rightful importance. Advertising through newspapers, magazines, placards, banners, radio and television is essential to draw the attention of the customers to their products. In this respect, India is perhaps as good as any other country now. Particularly the advertisements on T.V. are amusing, imaginative and catchy. With the exception of a very few which are below average, all the rest can be rated as 'good', 'very good' and 'superb'. Other methods of marketing like concept selling and niche correspondence too are fast catching up.

But advertisements could draw a customer to a product only once. To make him a permanant customer and also to influence him to recommend to his friends to use that product, it requires much more than a mere advertisement. The most important factors of a customer's consideration before making his choice of a product are (1) price (2) quality, (3) availability/proximity of the dealer's shop and (4) after-sales service. For items like soaps, toothpaste, detergent, generally the factors influencing a customer's choice are quality, availability and price in that order.

For items like cars, television sets, refrigerators and mixies, a customer would consider price, quality and after-sales service in that order, before making his choice. The choice of items like fertilizer, cement, textiles is made mainly on considerations of availability in the proximity and price. Thus depending on the nature of the product and the customer, the considerations on which one's choice is made differ very much. The persons engaged in marketing of a product should keep this in view and lay accent on those aspects which constitute the main criteria for a customer to make his choice.

No doubt, even in the present day sellers' market in our country, several prize/gift schemes, easy instalment schemes for payment, off-season reduction sales etc are being offered for some items from time to time to attract more customers and to avoid loss on account of accumulating inventories. These schemes are in tune with those followed in the developed countries where the market conditions are favourable to the customers. But these schemes should be extended to many more items and should be available always.

Suppose there are 25 producers for a popular product and their total production is 12½% more than the estimated demand. Then unless, everyone of the producers keeps up the quality and price more or less on par, there is a possibility of 3 or 4 of them being forced out of business. But if every producer is as good as another in maintaining quality and price of his product, the surplus stock left out with each one of them at the end of a year will be less than 1/2% of the overall demand or about 5% to 15% of his own production and as such it would not have any serious impact on his business financially. In such an ideal situation, the producers will be constantly on the alert with regard to the customer's needs. Marketing department plays a key role in every organisation in keeping the number of its customers sufficient to buy its product to an extent that ensures the organisation a handsome profit. Even an occasional strike or reduction in the rate of production in one or two organisations due to any other reason would not affect the customers' interests. Surplus stocks within a limit could stimulate growth in demand also. But, if the 25 producers could produce only 75% of the total requirement, the customers would stand to lose because the producers are likely to become complacent about the quality and they may also raise the prices in view of the demand exceeding the supply by a large percentage.

Because of the scarcity conditions and relative poverty of the rural people, the vast market potential in our villages remains largely untapped till now. The marketing Managers should take time off to turn their attention to this vast market. If individuals cannot buy items like cars, television sets and VCR's the village Punchayats or groups of people could be persuaded to buy them for their collective use. Even many individuals/families may be in a position to buy them. But they would not have thought of buying them as the marketing staff of the Companies are too far away from them. Items like cycles, mopeds, cassette players should be made available to the rural people at dealer-outlets located as near to their villages as possible.

If, indeed, India has to catch up with the developed countries in their living standards by the turn of the century, we should ensure that every village is connected by a motorable road, provided with Electricity, drinking water, a school, a post office, a hospital, a few telephones, TV sets and taxies. If this is aimed at, besides the development of the villages, a tremendous growth of industries too could be ensured.

Marketing departments would have to work hard right from now in this vast market on forecasting the demand for their products, formulating attractive schemes for their sales, ensuring facilities for after-sales service and creating the awareness among the rural people about the advantages of the use of their products/services.

10

Planning and Management of Construction Projects

In our country, there are very few construction projects which have been completed as per the original time schedule. The delay in completion is, to a large extent, contributing to the overrun in the cost as well as to delay in the succeeding operations. This situation has become so common that people have taken such delays for granted as of routine nature. But it should be noted that these delays can be considerably minimised - may be eliminated altogether - with better project planning.

Tenders: It has become a practice to call for tenders even before the project is properly planned. Only a few indicative drawings showing the general layout of the project are enclosed with the tender. As the detailed drawings are not made, the quantities of work mentioned in the tender will be very approximate. The specifications of most of the works are left quite vague.

Time for submission of tenders: In most of the projects, the time given for the submission of tenders is too short. This makes it very difficult for the tenderers to study the site conditions, ascertain the availability of materials, their prices and the details of work in the project. As a result, quite often the tenderers will fill the tenders hastily working out their rates arbitrarily trying to err on the safe side. Some of the clients seem to think that the contractors would have no other work on hand at the time they call for tenders and they would be able to devote their full attention to their tenders only.

Conditions in the tenders: The conditions in the tender documents are so stringent that an ordinary but otherwise able and sincere contractor will find it hard to fulfil. For instance, every tender is required to be accompanied by an Earnest Money Deposit, very often in the form of a Bank Guarantee. A contractor may have to submit several - may be ten or more - tenders before he could get one contract. How many contractors could afford to bear the financial charges without feeling (buckling under) the strain? Won't the contractors include these charges in their rates, while submitting their tender, thus boosting up the rates? In this process, the only beneficiaries are the bankers.

In fact, when a tender is called, the Employer is reasonably certain that a suitable contractor could be selected from among the tenderers, whereas except one all the other tenderers will be unsuccessful. Therefore, just as an Employer pays the travelling and other expenses to the candidates appearing for an interview for a job, the Employer in the case of Projects should announce that he would pay a certain fixed amount (this could be very nominal, to start with, varying from Rs.1000 to Rs.10000/- depending upon the cost of the project) to the unsuccessful tenderers whose tenders are submitted in prescribed form and found to be valid. Incidentally, this will discourage the tendency of some departments/organisations calling for tenders frivolously and shelving the projects indefinitely thereafter.

There was a time when the contractors were not being paid any mobilisation and machinery advance at all. But now, the times have changed and in almost every project, mobilisation advance is being given to the contractor. At times (particularly in the case of companies in Private Sector), while calling for quotations for the supply of manufactured items no earnest money deposit is stipulated. If it is feared that a civil contractor may backout after the submission of a tender, why can it not be thought that the suppliers of manufactured items can as well back out? It should be remembered that no contractor with a reasonably good standing submits his tender frivolously just for the fun of submitting a tender. If any tenderer backs out when the contract is awarded to him, he will very soon lose his reputation and may have to go out of contract business. Therefore a serious rethinking is called for in respect of Earnest Money deposit.

There are a host of other forms to be filled in like the list of machinery, man power, works completed, works on hand, financial viability etc, which are enough to sap the enthusiasm of the up and coming or even experienced contractors. In many cases, either these lists are furnished without relevance to facts or they are not read and taken seriously by the clients. In a few tenders, it is required of the tenderers to give the names of the personnel intended to be posted for that project and their bio-data. Surely, it goes beyond one's comprehension as to how any tenderer can think of specific personnel to be posted at a work site even before submitting the tender and without having any idea about his chances of getting the work.

At times, the clients are so unreasonable and fastidious that the experience of even a well established contractor in the construction of large cement plants, fertilizer factories & automobile factories is not good enough in their view for issue of a tender for, say, the construction of a thermal power plant! They insist on the tenderers having experience in their type of project and in that geographical region!

Some other conditions in the tenders sound quite funny. The employer or his consultant reserves the right to reject any material or work at any stage before the completion, not withstanding the fact that it has been approved by him earlier. They also reserve the right to reject any or all the tenders without assigning any reason therefor, although the tenderers would have spent a lot of their time and money in submitting the tender. The employer and the consultant take no responsibility for the subsoil data furnished with the tender. The contractor is required to ascertain the correctness of the data within the short time before submitting his tender. Such conditions make a mockery of the whole system of calling for tenders. The tenderers also are now-a-days taking such conditions lightly. Almost impossible targets are fixed for completion of the work, with a clause of liquidated damages attached to the same. In quite some cases the contractor adds the maximum leviable liquidated damages to his rates in the tender. If luckily, the liquidated damages are not levied, he will benefit to that extent. Otherwise, he will pay the money for which he has already made provision in his rates.

Time for deciding on the tenders: The clients and consultants take an unduly long time to evaluate the tenders. Some private companies won't even open the tenders for several weeks after their submission. In Government and public sector projects, the tenders are generally opened on the last date fixed for submission of the tenders but thereafter they take their own time for evaluation. Instead, if they give a few more weeks to the tenderers for submission of tenders, and take a little less time for evaluation of the tenders, it would go a long way in ensuring the tender rates being more realistic and avoidance of a lot of delay. The practice of post-tender negotiations should be discouraged, even if it cannot be dispensed with altogether. The tenderers will quote more reasonably if they know that they will not get a chance to review the rates.

Possibility of malpractices by the clients to give the contract to a pre-determined contractor by manipulation can be minimised.

One more genuine grievance of the tenderers is that the result of the tenders or the P.Q. (Pre-qualification) applications is not communicated to them. Some clients (especially Government organisations) refuse to furnish the results of the tenders when those who could not attend the opening of the tenders ask for the same. They say that the tenderers should be present while the tenders are opened or should gather the details from other tenderers who might have attended the meeting. The least that the clients could do in fairness to the tenderers for all the trouble they have taken in submitting the tenders, is to inform them individually in writing, the results of the tender after opening the tenders and the name of the contractor to whom the work has been awarded.

Acquisition of land: In a few projects, the acquisition of the land on which the structures have to be built would not have been anywhere near completion before the tenders are called.

Drawings: It is a wonder as to why the project planners do not get all the working drawings ready at least by the time the tenders are finalised. There are a large number of projects where the progress has suffered considerably, because of non-availability of the working drawings in time. It is wrong to think that the drawings could be supplied as and when the work progresses. If all the drawings are given before the commencement of work, the contractor will have a clear picture of the project and he can programme the construction to suit his resources, of course giving priority to the portions required by the client earlier. In that case, the consultant will be left with the task of only giving clarifications in the drawings and supplementing details wherever they are missing.

Cement and Steel: The client should make arrangements for procurement of cement and steel well in advance. In view of the prevailing scarcity condition in the market, the client should plan to procure at least 40% of the steel required for the project before commencing the work. Similarly, a minimum stock of cement required for 6 to 8 weeks should always be maintained.

Payments: Just as it is necessary that the contractors should carry out works maintaining good quality and speed, so is it imperative that the client should make payments promptly to the contractor on submission of his bills. In some organisations, the contractor is made to run from pillar to post before he can get the money against his bills. In Government and Public Sector organisations the delay could be due to shortage of funds. Sometimes delay could occur because the project officials get the work done before getting approval from competent authorities. In such cases the contractors have to suffer, though it is no fault of theirs. In some private companies the accountants will check each bill as if it were the final bill, thereby causing abnormal delays in payments. There are also instances of some projects being started without making arrangement for sufficient funds and getting necessary approvals. As a result, the projects are stopped half way through, causing heavy loss to the contractors. It should be stipulated that such losses are made good by the clients.

However, in spite of all these difficulties, some clever contractors are succeeding in making handsome profits by providing amply for all these factors in their rates or by managing to get away with chunks of money in supplementary claims.

Although the tender conditions appear to be very strict, in most cases, they are watered down, giving the benefit of doubt to the contractor. In some rare cases, of course, the contractors are harassed applying the conditions of the contract, to the letter.

Perhaps, the following norms may be adopted in order to get over the above problems.

(i) Before calling for tenders, the acquisition of most of the land, if not all should be completed (ii) Almost all the working drawings should be got ready by the time the contract is awarded (iii) The specifications should be clear cut without leaving scope for the contractor to give a different interpretation (iv) A minimum of 4 weeks time should be given for submission of tenders. Where know-how of foreign technology is involved, the time should be extended to 6 weeks. In the case of very large projects, even still longer time should be given (v) The tenders should be evaluated within 8 weeks, as far as possible (vi) The conditions regarding Earnest Money deposit should be deleted. This practice has become too out-moded and is causing a lot of financial strain to the contractors. (vii) The contractors should be asked to submit a brochure or a 'resume' about their organisation instead of being asked to submit data in different formats (each client has his own formats), sometimes with the attestation of former employers or bankers. Membership of bodies like the "Builders' Association of India" should be considered as a sufficient proof of the contractors' credentials. Such organisations may enrol contractors in categories like A,B,C, etc. according to the members' technical and financial capabilities. (viii) The client should procure at least 40% of the steel required for the project by the time he asks the contractor to commence the work. He should also arrange to supply the "inserts" and "embedments" falling within his scope of work well in time to avoid interruption of work. (ix) cement required for the work of 8 to 10 weeks should be stored at site by the client. (x) Prompt payments should be ensured for the work done. (xi) In spite of all these facilities, if a contractor fails in delivering the goods, the client should have the right to review after the lapse of 50% of the time allotted for the project where the duration is less than 18 months and to cancel the contract if it is felt necessary. The review can be made after the lapse of 9 months or 30% of the time (whichever is higher) where the duration of the project is longer, (xii) Similarly, if the clients delay the payments or release of drawings or supply of cement and steel, the contractor shall have the right either to put in his claim for compensation of his loss or to withdraw from the contract (xiii) A team consisting of the representatives of the client, consultant and the contractor should hold monthly meetings to review the progress and to thresh out the points of dispute and claims on each other, if any. This team should be encouraged to work in a spirit of cooperation instead of confrontation. They should refer points on which they have difference of opinion to a sole arbitrator, with stipulation that the award should be given within 4 weeks. Except in very rare and justified cases, old claims of the months already covered should not be pursued. (xiv) Last, but not the least, the programme should be drawn up realistically allowing reasonable time for each activity, taking into consideration the nature of the work and site conditions.

If these points are observed meticulously, very few projects will get delayed. The strain on the contractors will be reduced. The possibility of disputes and unreasonable claims of the contrators can be eliminated to a large extent.

11

Pollution Control in Towns and Cities

It is indeed interesting to note that Surat is now rated as one of the cleanest cities in our country. A little over two years ago, in the wake of an outbreak of plague, Surat was described as a town stinking with filth, garbage and sewage. Some of the scenes in the photographs published in newspapers and magazines at that time to illustrate the insanitary conditions there were so repulsive that many of the readers got a vomitting sensation on seeing them.

In the light of this background, naturally the news about Surat having become a clean city is as pleasing as its improvement is remarkable. The credit for achieving this should be given to the Municipal Staff and workers headed by the Municipal Commissioner, S.R. Rao. The people of the town also deserve appreciation, as without their co-operation, the transformation of a filthy place that it was into a clean and neat place now would not have been possible. All of them have proved the age old saying "where there is a will, there is a way". Instead of being resigned to their fate of living in shabby and unhygienic conditions, they have all worked with a rare determination and dedication for making their city, the envy of the other towns and cities in the country in the matter of cleanliness and hygienic conditions.

If all the cities and towns of our country follow the example of Surat, India's image abroad will be cleansed of the stigma of being unclean and unhygienic. Incidentially, the tourism industry will also grow by leaps and bounds. What is even more important is that the people will be healthier, being free from pollution.

For this to happen, the people and municipal authorities in the various towns and cities should take certain concrete steps. Let us take a city, say Delhi and examine what is needed to be done for achieving this goal.

First of all, the roads should be cleared of cattle, pigs and stray dogs. It is a pity that they are often encountered even on main thorough fares. They are not only causing disruption in traffic but also causing insanitary conditions. If only the traffic police and the Municipal staff are a little more strict, this menace can easily be eliminated.

The second thing to be done is to remove all the beggars and hawkers from the traffic junctions, pavements, sub-ways etc. They are proving to be a terrible traffic hazard. Vintage points on the pavements, in the sub-ways and at the places of worship are occupied by them right from the morning till late in the night. The pedestrians are put to a lot of inconvenience because of this.

The beggars touch every vehicle stopped at a traffic signal and pester the occupants for alms. Some of them suffering from deadly contagious diseases pose a danger of spreading their diseases to the unwary passers by. They are not only a nuisance but also an eyesore. No doubt, the beggars who are really incapacitated to earn a livelihood by any other means deserve sympathy. Such persons can be helped by the Municipal authorities and the Government by housing them in a separate colony and giving them a subsistence allowance. Those who want to give charity should put the money in "hundies" kept at various places and that money should be distributed to the beggars from time to time by the Municipal authorities.

Many areas in the city are stinking with garbage, sewage water etc. The Municipal authorities should divide the whole city into around 500 sectors and entrust each sector to a contractor for keeping it clean and neat. Such contracts should be given to the professional sweepers, themselves. The amount can be paid on a monthly basis, fixing the quantum on the size of the sector and the amount of filth to be cleared. If a contractor fails to keep his/her sector clean at the desired level, he/she should be replaced by giving a month's notice.

In some areas, the problems may be more deep rooted and may not be solved by a mere cleaning operation. For instance, the drains being too small or non-existent, the drainage water might be flowing on to the roads in some areas. In such cases, the Municipal authorities should take up the work of constructing new drains and/or enlarging the existing drains.

In each sector, a few local people, preferably retired persons should be nominated to caution the people throwing garbage on the roads and public places and to report to the Municipal authorities, if necessary. Stern measures like imposing punitive fines should be taken to discipline the people in this respect. The people passing urine etc. on the road-side should be punished severely.

Smoking is another menace causing irreparable damage to the smokers as well as the people around them. Although, it is stated that smoking could cause cancer and warnings that "smoking could be dangerous to health" are printed on the Cigarette packets, the rate of smoking or the number of smokers has not diminished.

One of the good ideas mooted by the Govt. of Delhi was to ban smoking in public places. But, alas, they have not taken any legislative measure so far to put the idea into action. By prohibiting smoking in public places, the pollution can be considerably reduced and the non-smokers can be saved from the ill-effects of passive smoking, that is, inhaling the air mixed with the tobacco smoke let out by the smokers. (Recently, an Act banning smoking in public places has come into force. But its implementation is unsatisfactory).

Slums are the other areas where the insanitary conditions abound. Getting the slums vacated is not an easy job. The Government should rehabilitate the slum dwellers by allocating land to them away from the city and providing them with minimum basic needs.

If the Government and Municipal authorities are vigilant, building of slums can be prevented. The rule to be followed in this case should be "prevention is better than cure".

The latest example of this kind is the effort of the West Bengal Government to evict the hawkers from the pavements of Calcutta in November, '96. The hawkers resorted to an agitation and the same was supported by some opposition parties for political reasons. Naturally, without showing alternative means of livelihood, throwing out several thousands of the hawkers overnight appears to be incorrect from the humanitarian point of view. However, if the Government was vigilant in the beginning itself and prevented the hawkers from occupying the space on pavements, this problem would not have assumed its present gigantic dimensions. In Chennai, a whole market named Burma Bazaar which has occupied all the pavement area near the Beach Station had to be legitimised later on, as the Government failed to take timely action in the beginning and by the time it woke up the problem became too big and complicated.

For the normal life of the people to be smooth, the traffic hurdles must be reduced to the minimum. The bad condition of the roads is not only causing greater wear and tear of the vehicles but also is slowing down the traffic considerably. It is surprising to note that often the bitumen roads are being repaired during the monsoon time. It is common knowledge that repairs carried out to tar roads during monsoon would not last long. Therefore, all road repairs should be completed well before the onset of rainy season.

It should be made compulsory for the vehicles to undergo periodical checks for the emission of obnoxious gases and carry certificates that the pollution emanating from them is within allowable limits. The traffic police should be satisfied with such certificates and should not harass the vehicle owners, as they are at times doing now with ulterior motives. They could inspect the pollution checking centres from time to time to ensure that bogus certificates are not given to the vehicles. If they feel that a vehicle is emitting too much of objectionable gases even though it has a valid pollution control certificate, they should direct the owner/driver of the vehicle to get it checked once again and report back at a specified police station within 24 hours with the certificate after a fresh test.

Finally, the pollution from the industries should be taken note of. In this case also, closing down all the industries at a time could lead to several problems of unemployment and short supply of the products/services. Therefore, this problem should be tackled in a phased manner, dealing with the most polluting industries in the first phase. As far as possible, the Government should help the industries in relocating themselves.

In this case also, the Government must prevent new industries springing up in residential areas instead of trying to remove them after they are allowed to be set up.

As far as the cleanliness of the city is concerned; the political parties should desist from fighting with one another and avoid working at cross purposes. For their temporary gains or with an eye on the so called vote banks, they should not allow creation of slums and setting up of industries in the residential areas, thereby endangering the health of the people.

These tips and remedies are equally applicable to all the other towns and cities of our country for making them as clean and hygienic as Surat.

12

Standardisation – Its Benefits to Industry

Thousands of years ago, when civilised life was unknown to man, his needs were very few and his interests were more or less confined to earning his livelihood. Slowly, by his innate urge for betterment of his conditions and ingenuity to use his intellect for great inventions, man has learnt to be civilised.

With the advent of civilisation, man has learnt to construct architectural and functionally convenient houses, and also many other things like laying roads, cultivation of lands, living a social life etc. With the advance of civilisation, man's interests in life went on multiplying into an astronomical number. Correspondingly, his needs also have become quite innumerable.

When man's needs were comparatively fewer till about the eighteenth century, many things required by him were made by the skill of hand. For instance, if a king of the olden days wanted clothes, they had to be woven by hand only. If a man wanted a knife, that had to be manufactured by the blacksmith of the locality either according to his requirements or the blacksmith's will. That is, things used to be produced according to the conception of the makers or, in some cases, the requirements of the fastidious customers. A defect of this system, apart from the slowness of production is wide disparity in standard of products for various customers. Fear of punishment or hope of a reward or vanity for praise and appreciation could induce a weaver to use all his dexterity and skill in spinning the best quality yarn and weaving finest cloth for a king or a wealthy and opulent merchant or a man of high social status. The same attention may not be paid to a commoner and occasionally he may not get his money's worth.

However, after the advent of the industrial revolution, the rate of progress of man's achievements has become breathtaking. A century ago, it is hardly imaginable that anybody could have visualised with any degree of certainty, the present day inventions like the television, success in splitting the atom and thereby releasing boundless energy and incredible feats like landing on the moon. The changes in social order are also no less momentous.

There are now countless factories and industries all over the world. They produce all the things that are the daily requirements of the population of the world. With the progressively increasing demand, the production of almost all the things is growing by leaps and bounds.

Specifications

If we take the building industry, the things required for construction like cement, structural steel, mild-steel round bars, high strength ribbed steel bars, are manufactured in bulk by several factories. Similarly in the automobile industry the tyres, batteries, wheels, the chasis and body are manufactured by several producers. Likewise in the case of electricals, the bulbs, wires, plugs, switches, radios etc. are manufactured by different industrial units. Like this, from a small pin to a gigantic machine, innumerable things like bolts and nuts, G.I. sheets, electric motors are manufactured by several organisations. Unless some standardisation is effected, each factory may manufacture its products according to its own specifications or what is even worse, without any specifications at all.

For instance, in the field of cement industry, each manufacturer may maintain in his product different degrees of fineness, strength, contents of magnesia etc. To an ordinary user, all the different types of cement manufactured by the various factories, will appear to be just similar to one another. But the cement supplied by each manufacturer may vary widely in the quality from day to day. The variation in the quality may be more marked between the products of different manufacturers.

From the point of view of the use for which the material is required, standardisation has to be effected. By doing so, the product will be of a particular minimum quality. For instance in the case of cement, one can take it for granted that the cement being sold in the market conforms to certain minimum standards stipulated by the I.S.I. namely, that the specific surface is not less than 2,250 sq. cm. per gram, magnesia content is not more than six per cent, initial and final setting times are within the range of 30 minutes and 600 minutes, and that the cement will produce a strength of 115 Kgs/cm^2 when standard cement mortar cubes are tested at the age of three days. In the absence of any such standardisation, each manufacturer may supply cement of his own specification. That is, where the raw materials are of excellent quality and the plant is giving a very good performance, the cement produced may be of exceptionally high quality and may be giving consistently a high strength of 200 Kgs/cm^2 when standard cement mortar cubes are tested.

In a place where the impurities are very large, the magnesium content may be allowed to be of the order of 10%. Thus the user of cement will have to test the quality of cement, each time he buys it for any work. One cannot take the strength, fineness, setting time and any other property of cement for granted. Testing any product so often is very difficult, expensive and tedious. Where a R.C. work of comparatively routine nature is being carried out, the design may be based on the assumption that the concrete strength will be, say, 2,250 lbs/sq. inch, if a proportion of 1:2:4 is adopted. But if the properties of cement vary so often and so widely, it will be difficult to assume like this as the strength may be lower or higher according to the quality of the cement available in the market.

Another important advantage of standardisation is that replacement will be very easy. Let it be imagined that a large factory roof has been provided with A.C. sheets supplied by one manufacturer. After a few years a few of the sheets are found to have been broken. In the market the stocks of the A.C. sheets of the brand that were purchased earlier are exhausted. In such a case unless standardisation is there, it would be difficult to carry out the replacement as the sheets manufactured by other factories may be of different specifications. Hence standardisation is highly useful for the customer, as he will be sure of a minimum quality and standard of the products.

Advantages

Le us take any products like M.S. rounds, rolled steel sections, G.I. or A.C. pipes, sanitary ware, paints etc. in building industry. In every case, the advantages of standardisation are only too obvious. If the mild steel is specified to be of a certain quality to give a minimum ultimate tensile stress of 42 Kgs/ mm^2 the designers can easily assume a safe working stress for the steel rods.

However, if the manufacturers are given a free hand and permitted to manufacture steel rods with mild steel of their own specification, each consignment of rods has to be tested by the user to detemine its quality. In the case of R.S. joists, the sections of the various I.S.M.B., I.S.M.C., angles etc. have been standardised. That is, every manufacturer has to produce these sections according to those standards only.

If this were not insisted upon, sections of various sizes required for a work cannot be procured from more than one supplier as the sizes of sections of steel structurals supplied by the various manufacturers may not be the same. The design also becomes very cumbersome as for each section that is available in market, the properties like the weight per metre, moment of inertia of the section about the x and y axes, radius of gyration etc. have to be worked out. In the case of pipes the specials like a tee, a bend, an elbow, a reducer and a screw down bibcock, manufactured in one factory may not fit into a pipe supplied by a different manufacturer.

Quality of Material

But fortunately, because of the standardisation, all products coming into the market will conform to certain standards like the quality of the material, the sizes of the bore, the thread, the shape etc. There may at best be some difference between one pipe and another made by different manufacturers in the finish or the margin of safety (extent of being superior) above the minimum standard. Thus standardisation is very vital for industrial products.

If we look into a few more examples in fields other than building industry, the above points may get some more support. One shudders to imagine what might be the fate of a tourist in an automobile if the gasoline sold by each oil company is of a different quality in terms of its octane number, combustibility, density, viscosity etc. The automobile engine will be reduced to scrap if fuel of different varieties is used for its running. A car can be fitted with a Dunlop, a Ceat, Firestone, M.R.F., Mansfield, Goodyear or any other tyre according to availability and choice of its owner, simply because all tyres are manufactured according to particular standard dimensions. So is the case in respect of torch light and torch cells.

In the case of electrical equipment, if standardisation is not effected, a plug of an electric iron, and that of a radio purchased from two different producers may not fit into a plug socket purchased from a third source. If an electric bulb of Philips make is burnt, again a bulb of the same make will have to be used for replacement. However because of standardisation, any electric bulb burnt can be replaced by a bulb of any other make according to availability and the customer's choice. There are examples galore of this type illustrating the many advantages of standardisation.

Standardisation helps in price reduction also. Mass production is possible only in the case of standardised goods. If electric motors are to be made according to individual orders and the specifications contained therein, the manufacturers have to spend a good deal of their time, energy and talent in design and manufacture of the motors. However, if motors are manufactured according to standardised patterns and capacities of say, 10 H.P., 15 H.P. etc. and with standard armature windings etc. the men at work can do the job with greater skill and at a faster rate because of the constant repetition. The designers will have to look into the design aspect only rarely to effect any changes in pattern, windings, the magnet to be used etc. Thereby the rate of production can be increased which will be followed by the reduction in cost. In this case, the customer has to choose a motor of the nearest capacity to his requirement.

If the Electric supply for domestic use is made available at 230 V in one town and say 330 V or 130 V in another town, how difficult it will be for a person transferred from one town to the other is only too clear for any one to understand. For, a table fan that he might have purchased to work at the voltage of electric supply in one town may not work in the other town.

So, things that could be used in one place will not be useful in another place. Standardisation avoids such troubles.

Till quite recently, in different regions of the country different standards were being followed in weights and measures. While in Tamil Nadu a standard measure for rice was a "Padi", that in northern part of Andhra Pradesh was a "Kuncham". Similarly while the weight of sugar was measured in "seers" in one part, a "pound" was taken as a standard measure in some other part. Thus a man of one part finds it very difficult to understand weights and measures of another part of the country. For drawing a comparison of the cost index between different parts, it will be necessary to convert the weights and measures into common units every time.

Collection and compilation of the statistical data also become very difficult. Similarly if a stranger happens to be walking in the countryside and enquires of a villager as to how far the next village is, he will be told that the next village is, so many 'Krose' from there. A krose is a unit in distance generally used in the northern part of Andhra Pradesh. A person from any other part will fail to make out anything from that expression. Standard units like a litre, kilogram, kilometer etc. adopted all over the country will eliminate such ticklish situations.

Cost of Product

Another point of importance and significance is that the consumer can check the costs of the various products more easily and the possibility for being misled or duped becomes much less. If there is a large difference in the price of two products, say H.T. wires, having the same minimum standards, the consumer will easily notice this and will find the causes for the difference. On the contrary, if no standardisation is implemented, the difference in prices will be attributed to several doubtful causes like superior quality, finish etc. There is every chance for some deceiptful producers to cheat customers by overpricing their products or supplying substandard and spurious goods. Thus the standardisation helps the customer in ensuring the quality and reasonable price of the products.

Standardisation safeguards the interests of manufacturers or sellers also in many ways. Quite often we hear customers grumbling about the quality of the things they buy. In the case of cement they may say after using the cement, that the cement is poor in quality. But the bulk of the customers do not know how to express their opinion in concrete and specific terms.

Thanks to the standardisation, it is easy for the cement supplier to convince the cement user about the quality of cement by conducting the necessary tests. In the same way there might be vague and ambiguous complaints about the quality of things like R.C. hume pipes, cast iron pipes, stoneware pipes, glasses, textiles etc. But if the standards for these items are defined in terms of measurable characteristics like length, diameter, thickness, strength and other attributes it would be easy for the suppliers to clear the wrong impressions of the buyers about the quality of these products. Likewise the prudent consumers would study these standards and show specific defects in the products, if they fall short of the standards.

Thus the standards will form the basis for judging a product to be good or bad; superior or inferior. On the contrary if such standards are not specified, difference of opinion about the quality of products may arise far too often. One may speak appreciatively about the quality of a product like fertilisers or infant food and his friend may disagree with him to that extent that he may use all his powers of rhetoric and argument to pin point what he considers as deficiencies in that product to make him "think his swan a crow". The same is not likely to happen if the opinion is to be expressed with reference to the standards set for the product. The manufacturer knows what is required of a product and the customer knows what to expect of the same. This will avoid unnecessary friction between them.

Because of the importance attached to such standards, great care should be exercised in formulating the standards so that they would be realistic, practicable and conforming to the requirements of the products. Where it may not always be possible to achieve a particular standard exactly, tolerances have to be allowed determining the same by applying statistical theories using averages and standard deviations. A good example of this is the weight of a cement bag. Although a cement bag should contain 50 kg of cement, it is almost next to impossible to pack the bags exactly to this weight even with the most sophisticated packing machine. Unless a tolerance is allowed in this weight, numerous litigations may arise between the buyer and seller.

Any product containing the mark of standardisation like the "I.S.I." in India can generally be relied upon as of a minimum prescribed standard. But it is also important for the organisation responsible for specifications for such standardisation in the products to exercise strict vigilance to check whether some manufacturers are unscrupulously using the mark of standardisation without really keeping their product upto the minimum standard.

Standards

Such articles not conforming to the standards but bearing the mark of I.S.I. or other symbol of standardisation will only shake the faith of the customers in the standardisation mark. However, if the I.S.I. mark is used conscientiously by all manufacturers on their products after ensuring the quality of the product to conform to the given standards, it will provide a useful guide to the customer in the choice of the goods.

Indeed he is spared a good deal of brain racking and

hesitation, once he acquires confidence about the quality and reliability of goods bearing the mark of such standardisation. Summing up, it can be stated that standardisation is a "sine qua non" for the orderly and systematic growth of industries, for the quality and relaibility of the products and for safeguarding the interests of and keeping harmony between the producer and user or seller and buyer.

Note: This chapter consists of an article written by this author in the year 1971. Therefore some of the standards of cement etc. referred to in this chapter may not be the same as the prevailing standards, at present.

13

Steps for the Reduction of Accidents

Every one is familiar with the old adage "A stitch in time saves nine" and also the proverb "Prevention is better than cure". "Accidents are often caused and seldom happen". These and similar sayings can be quoted to drive home to one and all the necessity to follow the rules of safety in industrial undertakings as indeed in anything we do in our daily routine.

The desire for personal safety and to guard oneself against possible danger is not something quite new to man. Even the brave and intrepid soldier of the ancient times, full of pride and impetuosity and willing to lay down his life cheerfully for the sake of his country was never careless to go to the battlefield without a shield.

With the advent of the industrial revolution, many factories and workshops have been set up all over the world and machines are being used for the production of a host of things in this world. Automobiles, aeroplanes, ocean-liners which have facilitated fast communications are the products of the present day industries. Other products like television, radio etc. are serving as very enjoyable entertainment and information media. Modern machines also facilitate quick printing of news papers, weaving of cloth, solving complicated mathematical problems and doing countless similar seemingly difficult and time consuming things. Manufacture of building materials like cement in large quantities also is facilitated.

With all the great benefits that we derive from the industrial growth, we cannot afford to ignore its inherent risks also, however insignificant they may be. No one can deny that walking from one place to another is far safer than riding an automobile. For, there is absolutely no risk what-so-ever in walking, although it would be extremely strenuous and slow as compared to going by an automobile. But the automobile ride is risky – however remotely – as there is always a possibility of an accident. However the automobile being maintained in an excellent condition and the driver highly skilful, the risk of accident is reduced to an insignificant and negligible level with the result that the sure advantages of travel by an automobile far out-weigh the few remotely possible and most unlikely events like an accident. So the worth whileness of a travel by an automobile is directly linked to the effectiveness of the steps to avoid the possibility of an accident.

Strict Observance of Safety Rules

It is at times astounding to note how a failure to observe simple rules of safety either out of negligence or a sense of complacence could result in serious accidents. Indeed most road accidents could be traced to the driving on the wrong side of the road, driving in an intoxicated condition, exceeding the speed limit set for that section of road, ignoring a traffic signal at a junction or poor maintenance of the automobile itself so that either the brakes or lights or steering etc. are not in good condition. Although it is strictly forbidden to cross the railway lines within station premises except by foot over-bridges, we find most people doing the forbidden thing, running the risk of meeting with an avoidable accident.

It is stipulated that in workshops, the workers should tuck

their shirts into their trousers and the sleeves should be folded upto their fore arms. But if any one goes with loose garments around him ignoring the above rule, he is likely to run the risk of his garments getting caught in a running wheel or a roller of a machine. Similarly, while doing welding, one should protect his eyes with colour glass shield. If anyone fails to follow this safety measure, he runs a grave risk of an injury to his eyes. The worker in a foundry should have his feet well protected by suitable shoes and his hands by gloves. If a worker ignores this while at his work, he may find himself badly scalded before he could realise his folly. Likewise smoking in an oil godown ignoring the placard that -'smoking is prohibited" could result in the godown being gutted and reduced to ashes, one day. The carelessness of one-worker or an inspecting officer-in going inside a rotary kiln without wearing a helmet might cause him an avoidable head injury as a result of some loose bricks dropping from the lining work. The recklessness of one working with acids in a laboratory may cause serious burns on his skin or at least a hole in his clothing due to acid spilling.

Hence all those working in factories have to be extremely careful in following the safety rules to the very letter. A person using a wrong spanner (say a larger one) for tightening a nut may either do the job imperfectly or damage the nut badly and at times injure himself as a consequence of the possible slipping of the spanner.

Training Helps

One has to know his work thoroughly. The performance of a half trained person at a machine can very well be compared to the naive and dangerous attempt of a beginner (in swimming) trying to cross a deep and wide channel. Thus before a person is entrusted with a job, he should be given a thorough safety induction. Especially on hazardous jobs like mining, the drillers, blasters, foremen etc. must be given a very elaborate and extensive safety induction training, as otherwise the risks involved will be too great.

Design and Safety

Many possible accidents could be avoided by proper design of machines and work premises. If a staircase is built with steps having 6" tread and 10" riser just to save some space, it will become a potential place of accident even with all the care of those using it. On the other hand steps of 10" tread and 6½" riser will greatly diminish the possibility of an accident to the persons climbing up or descending down the staircase. A good buffer at the edge of the hopper into which limestone is to be dumped by means of tipping trucks may greatly reduce the possibility of the tipping trucks accidentally slipping into the hoppers. Providing suitable hand rails and toeboards for walkways at a high level, providing protective guards on the sides of limestone or coal carrying conveyor belts and a walk-over where they cross a road etc. will contribute much to the general safety of personnel and prevent untoward accidents.

Safety in Construction Work

In the construction of factory buildings also, risks can be greatly reduced by following rules of safety. While constructing a building. good scaffolding must be provided for the workmen to stand on and to keep the building materials for work. But if the scaffolding is badly designed or erected with decayed wood or rusted steel members in insufficient sections, the scaffolding may give way causing injury to those working on it as also to the passers-by. Sometimes, the shuttering of a R.C. slab or beam is removed much sooner than the stipulated time to hasten the progress of construction work. Once in a way, such early removal of shutters will cause serious failures of the structures causing damage to life and property. While stressing a pre-stressed concrete beam by posttensioning method, the risk of an occasional slipping of a H.T. wire is to be anticipated. If the workmen do not stand clear of the line of the wire being stressed, it may slip suddenly and pierce through the body of the person standing in its line. Thus certain fundamental rules of safety have to be observed to avoid risk of possible accidents. While working on an electrical line, the worker should first ensure that the mains are switched off and the electric wires positively earthed. Observance of such precautions go a long way in ensuring the safety of the workers and minimising the occurrence of accidents.

Production V/s. Safety

One wrong notion among many industrial workers and supervisors to be noticed is that they could achieve higher production by ignoring a few of the safety rules. For example they prefer to use a wrong spanner for tightening or loosening a nut because the right spanner is available at a few yards away and it would take sometime for fetching it. They would walk over a slippery floor instead of walking over a non-slippery walk-way because the latter would involve a larger distance by a few feet. We find huge weights being lifted by pulley blocks tied to the roof truss members although they are not designed for carrying these loads. Some people argue that these acts would entail only one per cent or 1/2 per cent risk. But according to the same theory, the probability of the accident occurring at the first time the safety rule is violated is just as good as its occurrence at the tenth or hundredth time of violation. Once an accident occurs, the working of the shop will be paralysed and temporarily thrown out of gear. The resultant loss of production will be far greater than the little increase in production that might have apparently been noticed as a consequence of skipping a few of the safety rules. Certain losses are too great for restitution, reparation or compensation. Hence everyone should be impressed about the absolute necessity of following the safety precautions.

Avoid Horseplay

The workers and supervisors must work with

concentration and while doing a job they should never allow their attention to be distracted. To ensure this, unauthorised people should not be allowed to visit the shops frequently. A congregation of the workers, debates, shouting etc. very close to another man working on a machine may cause a temporary diversion of his attention and involve him into an accident. Hence the workers and supervisors must conduct themselves with the utmost dignity and restraint and should not indulge in horseplay.

Proper Maintenance Ensures Safety

Last, but not the least, is the need for a thorough periodic check of the various machines, which is otherwise termed as maintenance. Most of the maintenance jobs are routine, repetitive and at times dreary and monotonous. Very often, when a machine is dismantled and reassembled or overhauled at the specified time, very few defects will be noticed requiring their special attention. Hence a tendency to take the things for granted creeps into the minds of the maintenance staff and they would not check each part of the machine as it should be according to the rules. Such acts of negligence may result in a serious accident once in a way. It must be understood that the maintenance job is intended to keep the machine in excellent working condition and to avoid even the remotest possibility of its breakdown while it is in use.

Conclusion

To reduce the incidence of accidents and to promote the safety in industrial units, the following measures should be taken.

1. The workers and Supervisors handling machines should be thoroughly trained to handle the jobs in the safest way.
2. The workers should use the right type of tools for doing the particular job.

3. They should strictly observe the stipulations regarding dress, footwear, gloves, goggles, life belts etc. for the various jobs that they are entrusted with.

4. They should avoid shortcuts in walking like, crossing over a conveyor belt or walking on a slippery floor or going too close to a running machine in preference to the ways intended for their walking.

5. Provide hand rails and toe boards for walk-ways at a high level and avoid steep staircases etc. while constructing factory buildings. After installation of a machine or its maintenance the guards over moving parts must be put back in position before it is allowed to run.

6. Provide good lighting for the workers to carryout their jobs without risk.

7. Offer incentives by announcing cash prizes to workers with accident-free record over certain stipulated period, of course linking this to the production also.

8. Pose of bravado, futile adventurism, risky impetuosity, clumsy slipshodness, disregard for safety rules on the part of workers must be strictly checked and sternly discouraged.

9. Catchy slogans, imaginative and realistic illustrations should be prominently displayed in the shops to attract the attention of the workers.

10. Lectures and screening of films impressing on the workers about the need for observing safety rules also will be helpful.

11. The machines in the factory should be designed with the safety aspect being taken as a prime consideration.

12. After every accident, the causes must be investigated

and suitable measures should be taken to prevent recurrence of such accidents. It is good to allow the person involved in an accident to describe how he was involved in the same and which are the safety rules he failed to observe.

13. Above all, it should be realised that a happy mind will greatly contribute to increase productivity and to eliminate accidents. The workers should never be upset while on their jobs. They should be given proper facilities for doing their work satisfactorily.

14. A well equipped first-aid room must be provided as close to the factory as possible.

Constant observance of the above is the price that we have to pay – a quid pro quo – for safety in industrial undertakings. But who would not pay this price gladly, for such desirable result and satisfactory return?

14

Requisites for an Executive to be Successful in construction industry

INTRODUCTION:

For success in any enterprise or a profession a methodical approach and a sincere and a ceaseless effort are necessary. Success by chance or a stroke of good luck is very rare. Many people might have been aware of the story of an astrologer by name, Midathambhatlu who rose to prominence by sheer luck. Just at that time a necklace of pearls was stolen in the King's Palace. When the search had proved futile, the King sent for the astrologer, having come to know about his fame. The king ordered the astrologer to find out the necklace within a week, threatening to have the astrologer's nose and ears cut off if he failed to locate the necklace. Being aware of the hollowness of his own knowledge, the astrologer was sure that the time had come when his bluff would be called. He sat in a room and was weeping aloud "OH MY NOSE AND EARS". Two maid servants in the King's Palace with the names "MUKKU AND CHEVVU" MEANING "NOSE AND EAR" who had actually committed the theft were curious to know what the astrologer was doing. When they heard the astrologer saying "OH MY NOSE AND EAR", the guilty maid servants thought that the astrologer had found out their guilt. They fell prostrate before the astrologer and confessed their guilt. The astrologer heaved a sigh of relief at this unexpected and favourable turn of events. He got rich rewards from the King by telling him where the necklace could be found. But such occurrences in real life are very rare indeed.

If anyone wants to be a successful executive in any field, he/she has to possess or cultivate certain qualities which are considered especially desirable. A few of the requisites which could contribute greatly to the success of an executive in construction industry, in contractors' organisations are mentioned below:

Should not be dogmatic

Set notions about men, material, equipment, work and related matters could cause hindrance to progress. One executive may have a poor opinion about the equipment of a particular make. He would first of all try to avoid that equipment at his work site. If by chance that equipment is forced to be used, he will attribute all the delays to that particular equipment only, without applying his mind to set it right. All his aversion for that participar equipment could have been the result of his own experience with that equipment at another worksite or hearsay. In the same manner he may behave in respect of a person or a material causing needless problems.

Should be impartial to staff

One should not align oneself with any faction. It is most important for an executive to build up an image for himself as an impartial person. Quite a few run into rough weather because of identifying themselves with one group or the other from considerations like caste, language, similarity in views on some matters or submissiveness. They turn a deaf ear to complaints on any one in the group. Some people in the group could misuse this positon to their own advantage. The people outside this group may get a feeling of frustration and fail to give their best and loyal performance.

Should be polite but firm where necessary and be friendly with people

Some people think that they can establish their superiority by shouting only. When they go to work site they call all those working around and give a thrashing to each one of them for no obvious reason. This becomes such a routine thing that people would give very little importance to such shoutings in due course. They try to avoid meeting such officers. For example if somebody comes to an executive with an application for leave when the work is in full swing, his answer to him should, of course be "NO". But he should explain the position patiently and in a friendly manner and he may finally refuse to grant the leave. Such an approach will not leave any unpleasant impression in the minds of the people. Friendliness and warmth will create good-will.

Should encourage people to come out with new ideas — One should not think good ideas are anybody's monopoly

Many people at top level think it below their dignity to accept new ideas from lower levels. Often people at lower levels are so much ridiculed at or suppressed that their faculties for thinking are considerably eroded. They will feel diffident about their own abilities. An executive should remember that at times some bright ideas may be thrown up from unexpected quarters.

Should appreciate good work

One should never feel hesitant to appreciate a person if he has done a good work. A word of appreciation for hard work or meritorious work of a person could prove to be a fine incentive for showing his mettle in further work.

Should guide the people rather than criticise their work. One should understand the problems

Some people often indulge in vociferous criticism but it will not contain any suggestions for improvements or for avoiding the mistakes. Rather than being content with finding faults, they should try to guide as to how the work can be done in a better way. Their approach should be to understand the problems rather than under-rating them or turning a blind eye to them.

Should plan the requirement of materials and machinery well in advance

Executives might have often come across situations when the fixing of reinforcement is delayed for want of binding wire because the requisition for the procurement of binding wire comes only after the entire stock is exhausted. Similarly a few times the vibrators have to be stopped for want of petrol, because it was not planned to keep a minimum stock of petrol always. Many times a concreting work could have been delayed because the requirement of metal, sand, cement etc. was not properly assessed before-hand. This kind of delays could be avoided if a little planning is done and the requirement of materials and machinery is projected well in advance.

Should prepare programmes for work

Whether a work is progressing fast or not can be assessed only when the rate of progress is compared with a programme. Only when a programme is made it will be known when a particular item of work is to be started or where a little more effort is needed to make up for delay. Therefore one should make it a point to have a programme for every work.

Should report the progress and problems to H.O.

Always one should remember that there is the H.O. to coordinate the work at various work sites. One should therefore promptly report to H.O. daily/weekly/monthly/or at other intervals the progress of work and any problems that one may be facing. One should never try to work in isolation. One should welcome suggestions and guidance from all quarters.

Should have a rapport with the Government Department/ Clients' Engineers

This is very essential because the civil work is such that any one can find some mistake or other if he wants to. Some times the department creates problems with some ulterior motives and not necessarily from their anxiety for good work. The executives should give a feeling that they are promptly attending to the remarks of the Department Officers. But they should also make it clear that unreasonable actions of the Department will be contested. Generally it can be assumed that half the problems at site are solved, once an understanding is reached with the Department.

Should safe-guard the interest of the Company

In the anxiety to create good-will in the Department, the interests of the company should not be lost sight of. For instance a Department Engineer may find himself in an embarrassing position to allow a particular extra item of work because he might have got it done without necessary approvals. In such a case if the amount involved is fairly large, one should try to put up the claim. Similarly in transacting business with other parties, the legitimate interest of the company should be his prime consideration.

Correspondence must be to the point rather than devious — Promptness is important

There used to be a Senior Officer who was never replying to any letter unless at least two reminders were given. When asked to explain his attitude, he replied with a mischievous smile that if he replied to the letters without any reminders people would think that he has got no other work. He wants them to know that he is busy. Secondly, if there is no reminder for a reply, the letter is not important enough to be replied to! One should never follow his example. Some people write long replies often missing the main point to be answered. While drafting a reply it is always good to be brief and clear.

Should maintain dignity and build the image of the Company

Very often engineers feel that by cringing before their superiors or departmental engineers, they can ensure appreciation for themselves. But such an attitude will put them in an awkward position. Once accustomed to such attitude it becomes very difficult to change at a later date. Cringing and over-obedience cannot make up for deficiencies in knowledge, work, promptness and agility. By doing so, not only their diginity is lost but the company's image also may be lowered. Company's image can best be preserved by doing the work as per programme and maintaining good quality.

Accuracy in work is more important than mere progress in some areas

There are some works like the gate grooves in a barrage or bolt holes in a machine foundation where accuracy is very important. If any error is made in works like this, rectification will take a lot of time. In such works accuracy is more important than mere progress. But it is not so in other works like a counterfort retaining wall or a cable tunnel in a factory. While it is not right to advocate deliberate mistakes and carelessness in doing these works, a little allowance in line, plumb, etc. may be given if those portions are going to be covered up with earth. The exposed face of the retaining wall and the inner faces of the cable tunnel should however be finished neatly to correct dimensions and ensuring accuracy in line, level and plumb.

Should not overburden the staff – understand their difficulties

At times some people say that they are working 16 hours or so in a day. But except in very rare cases, no one will be able to work for more than 8 hours in a day, consistently. On any particular day, one might have worked for 12 hours or more but on the very next day, he/she might be able to work only for 6 hours. But, many people fail to note this fact. Even if somebody wants to or is forced to work for 12 hours a day regularly his out-put and efficiency will very much be reduced. Therefore it is not fair to overburden the staff and to blame them for poor results. Instead, it is better to give limited work and expect a high degree of efficiency and standard. It is wrong to think of reducing cost of a project by cutting down man power. If anyone analyses the project cost, the wages of staff would not account for even 5%. Therefore, it would be wise to have about 10% surplus staff rather than running the show with deficient staff. This will take care of the eventuality of some staff suddenly going on leave during working season or resigning the job for better prospects.

Should not sacrifice quality, for, it does not cost much more but it will spoil the image

In an industrial multi storeyed building, if the plumb of a column is out by a few centimeters, it is worth delaying the work by a few minutes to set right the shuttering rather than starting the concreting just for showing progress. The column being out of plumb will cast a permanent reflection on the ability of the contractors. Their image will be tarnished. By not rectifying the shuttering in time, neither any saving in cost is achieved. Similarly the quality of concrete may be badly affected if the mixing is not done for the minimum prescribed time or compaction is not done properly. If the engineers at site ignore this, the concrete may show up defects or may fail at a later date. This may cast a slur on the name of the contractors.

Rates should be quite workable Otherwise no contract could succeed

The ultimate object of any contract work is to make a handsome profit for the company. But, if unworkable rates are quoted just for getting the contract by hook or by crook, it will become a difficult task for the engineers at site to make both ends meet. Therefore a good deal of thought should be given to the cost of material, labour, hire charges of machinery and other incidental charges while quoting the rates.

Claims should be put up in genuine cases – Frequent and frivolous claims could tarnish the image of the company

A joke published in a paper illustrates this point succinctly. Once a watch shop owner told his son that he has bought 100 watches at Rs. 100 each. He asked his son to sell them at Rs.98/- a piece. The young man was surprised and asked his father how they can make a profit if they sell the watches at less than their cost price. The elder man answered that their profits will come from the repair of these watches! Once a company is known for putting up frivolous claims, the prospective clients try to avoid giving works to them. However, where there is a genuine reason for a claim, by all means it should be pursued. Frivolous and untenable claims should be avoided to the extent possible. Once the clients were surprised when a contractor requested the soil strata at 5 m. below ground level to be classified as "soft disintegrated rock" whereas the clients have classified it as "hard rock requiring blasting". The reason for the contractor to classify the soil as soft disintegrated rock was that there was no rate for the soil of that classification and treating it as a new item of work he asked for almost double the rate for excavation in hard rock! Of course, not only his requrest was not granted, but also his contract was ultimately terminated due to many other reasons.

Should be thorough with tender conditions

It pays well if the engineers study the conditions of tender with due care. Many unreasonable actions of the department can be contested if the contractors are thorough with the conditions.

Should study the drawings

An executive should know the main features of the work.

Unless one studies the drawings one may not have clear conception of the work. The drawings must be read thoroughly.

Should be in touch with latest developments in technology and management techniques

If one does not know about slip form technique one may plan to concrete the side wall of a tall silo using conventional shuttering. Where an excavator can be used for excavation, manual labour may be used out of ignorance. In such cases, the results will be delay in work, increase in cost and the unseemly and clumsy sight. It is advisable that the Executives go through technical journals regularly and attend seminars and training courses occasionally.

Bills should be prepared neatly and in time

Billing is just as important as the construction work. For bills to be passed in time, they should be prepared neatly enclosing all necessary statements like cement and steel consumption and stock, secured advances etc. People having experience and aptitude in this work should be employed for the preparation of bills.

Finance

The work should be planned taking into account the finance available and the cash flow. Grandiose planning is bound to fail if commensurate funds are not available. The motto of wisdom "cut the coat according to the cloth" should be followed scrupulously. An executive's standing in the eyes of staff will be considerably improved if he can ensure prompt payments to the staff, labour and sub-contractors.

Record must be maintained neatly

At many work sites if one goes to a mixer operator and asks how many bags of cement have been consumed for the day's work, he would scratch his head and start counting the empty gunnies. If a note book is maintained by him and he ticks off a number after every mix, this situation can be avoided. Records should be maintained about the quality and quantity of work done on each day, the stoppage of work or queries raised by department etc. for future reference. These records will be of immense value in quoting for future works or putting up claims etc. Computers should be used for keeping accounts and other records.

Freedom to work without fear

Some people think that a fear complex will keep people on their toes and spur them to do the work sincerely. But it should be noted that fear complex could kill the innovative spirit also. It must be believed that by and large people are sincere and are willing to work. Executives have only to give guidance and create the necessary congenial atmosphere. If a person is under a constant threat of disciplinary action from his superiors or the department, he will not be able to give a good account of himself.

Should share the credit with others

One should not be a boss, but a leader. Whenever a work is done satisfactorily either ahead of schedule or conforming to quality, some people at higher level snatch the credit for themselves. If they are generous and share the credit with the people lower down who have toiled so much for the work to be done satisfactorily, their morale will be boosted. They will work with renewed vigour and interest in future works.

Safety in work should be insisted upon

Safety should be always given maximum importance in any project. From time to time people should be cautioned about the need to observe safety rules. Always it should be remembered that an accident could delay the work considerably apart from causing misery to the concerned person and his family.

Above all, a manager at site could succeed only if he enjoys full confidence of the H.O. and this is amply evident to the staff and the Deptt.

Nowadays, people respect power and position more than knowledge and efficiency. Therefore it is very essential that the H.O. makes it clear to the company staff and the department that the executive at site enjoys their full support, if they want the Executive to prove his worth.

CONCLUSION

It is hoped that these tips will help the executives at work sites of contractors in improving their style of working and thereby the overall performance of all concerned in their projects. Perhaps it will result in better quality of work and speedier completion of the projects.

15

Economic Policies and the Common Man

Economic policies of the Government have an effect on everyone in the country in one form or the other in varying degrees. The same cannot be said about the policies in any other area. Still, it is surprising that there seems to be a greater awareness among the people about the policies on political matters, religious affairs and social problems, if one has to judge from their reactions by way of mass demonstrations etc. Often, it is found that it is much easier for a Government to take decisions of such far reaching consequences like the devaluation of a currency or imposing taxes or liberalising imports and exports than to demarcate afresh the boundaries of a state or to resolve an issue like the Babri Masjid and Ram Janma Bhoomi Temple. The reason for this is that the people are better informed about and more easily excited on matters of political and religious nature. But very little is being done to educate the common man about the implications of the economic policies of a Government in so far as their daily lives are concerned.

Much of the discussions on economic policies is confined to the so called intellectual circles only. The few articles and books published on such subjects are written with such statistics and terminology that a common man would not be able to make either head or tail of them. Articles written in all languages in plain and simple words spelling out clearly what the merits and disadvantages in a policy and how it is going to affect the vast majority of the people in the short, medium and long terms would help create the desired awareness among the people at large.

After Independence, our Government pursued an economic policy aimed at creating a Socialistic pattern of society. Emphasis was laid on developing industries and strengthening the public sector. In the successive five year plans, many projects were taken up covering many fields like Agriculture, Health, Education and Science and Technology. There is no doubt that our country has taken rapid strides of development in most of these areas although it should be conceded that much more could have been achieved with greater efficiency, less wastage, better planning and with more committment in reducing corruption. The abnormal rise in population too proved to be a big hurdle.

Although one should not be rigid about the day to day policies, certainly one should not lose sight of the very objectives and the goals set to oneself, while making any changes to suit the needs of the time. Taking into account the winds of change blowing over many countries in East Europe and the former Soviet Union and the like and also the then prevailing critical situation in our foreign exchange reserves, increasing inflationary rate etc; our Government has made sweeping changes in our economic policies. Let us take a look at the outcome of these policies.

Now it has become easier for importing and exporting goods, technology, services etc. We are now encouraging foreign investment in industry and business in our country. We are allowing the foreign investor even to have control of the industry and business. Another important aspect of this policy is to encourage privatisation of industry and business and to disinvest the Government shares in some of the public sector units, particularly those incurring losses regularly. Doubtless, these policies have helped in getting over our immediate problem with regard to foreign exchange reserves. But we should think of the likely effect of these policies in the medium and long terms.

Let us discuss as to what are the reasons for the public sector to fail where the private sector succeeds. In the public sector, the employees have job security and perhaps this may be a reason why their output is, more often than not, far less than their capacity. This is further aggravated because of the lack of accountability. The interference of the Government in the day to day functioning of the public sector units and hindering effective decision making and management are also major causes contributing to the inefficiency and low productivity in many of the units. In a private sector unit, these defects are minimised to a great extent. For achieving a particular financial gain, the management and officials of private sector companies are going all out and are not hesitating even to adopt certain short cuts and devious methods which the public sector units can not adopt. Therefore, the Government should look into the problems of the public sector units and find solutions for them with a view to making those units viable and serve the purpose for which they were established instead of resorting to summary disinvestment and depending on private sector for everything. Barring a few of the major industrial groups, the rest of the private industrial units are run by a few individuals or a single family and the whole future of the industrial or business unit depends on those individuals and families. Many a time, the sudden exit of such individuals or differences within the family has played havoc on the working of an industrial or business unit in the private sector leaving the employees in a lurch and causing loss and inconvenience to its suppliers and customers. At least, this kind of problems are non-existent in the public sector units. If a board of management is appointed for each public sector unit, offering the members an incentive for running the unit efficiently/profitably, the working of the public sector units could be improved. Misuse of power, nepotism, corruption and lethargy/inefficiency should be dealt with appropriately in a stern manner.

The efficiency of a unit cannot be always measured by the profit made. Profit can be increased by avoidance of taxes, compromise in quality of products/services and on higher pricing of the products/services in addition to minimising the cost of the organisation. Between private sector and public sector, the former is definitely better equipped to achieve these ends. But, then, who is the beneficiary? A few individuals or families stand to gain a lot at the expense of a large number of people, some of them employees and the rest of them customers.

There are some departments like posts and telegraphs and Railways. Government should perceive them as service organisations rather than profit making business enterprises. Let us take the case of the many courier service organisations in our country now. Their service is definitely not better than the speed post of the postal department of the Government. But the difference in their rates is so vast that the courier service organisations are literally minting money.

But alas! The messengers and the errand boys are paid a mere pittance as compared to the salaries and perks of the postmen in the Post and Telegraph Department. If only the Speed-post service has more post offices, the fleecing of the public in this area for the unreasonable and abnormal profit of a few can be minimised. If the Railways are handed over to the private sector many of the trains might be cancelled if there are no returns of profit from them. By this, only the public will suffer. The so called efficiency in the running of the trains will only help in filling the private coffers of a few individuals and families. If a Government is sincere and really means business, it is not so difficult to plug the loopholes in the working of the public sector units. One of the first things to be done in this direction is to award deterrent punishments to the corrupt persons and to confiscate 50% of their assets suspected to be illegally acquired as a first step pending further enquiry. Another factor that ails the Public Sector is the fabulous perks to their employees and the exhorbitant expenditure incurred on them. Once a PSU shows a high profit in one year, the management is revising the perks and salary grades of the employees. Even when it incurs loss in the subsequent years, it will not be able to reduce those perks. Some of the employees are claiming too much money in the form of medical benefits. The free passes to employees of Railways and Airlines should be reduced in number and should be valid in off-seasons only.

Once foreign investment goes beyond a limit, it will show its adverse effect on the political life of the country. Economic dominance is almost as bad as political dominance. To throw out a foreign investor at any future time, if such a step is warranted from the point of view of National interests, is not going to be an easy proposition.

The Government says that the rate of inflation has been brought down to nearly 7% from the then prevailing 16% in the last 2 years. It is no doubt creditable. But what counts most for the common man is the prices of his daily needs. He is not much bothered whether the prices of cars and V.C.R.'s have been reduced because of concessions given in the excise duty. He will be happy, if the prices of food, clothing and shelter are reduced or at least kept at a steady level. The increase in the bus and train fares has hit the people hard.

Talking about shelter, one cannot help commenting on the way the land prices are shooting up. A person of a middle income group would find it hard to save enough from his/her earnings in a life time even to own a house/plot in or around a city. Their prices are being hiked up by the real estate dealers every other day. Surely, the Government could do something to prevent the real estate dealers from making unreasonable profits. Some of them are buying land at throw away prices and are selling the same in the form of residential plots at astronomical prices. Why can't this be classified as black marketing? Why can't the Government fix a limit on the net profit in a deal to, say 15% and prohibit the sale of any piece of land for at least one year after its purchase? Such a step would definitely reduce the speculative purchases of land just for making huge profits.

The house rents also are sky high in urban areas. If the Government fixes a ceiling on the rent of a flat/house as a certain percentage of its original cost of construction etc. the house rents may come down substantially.

Every Government promises to provide employment to the educated youth. But their promises remain unfulfilled. If the Government is keen on providing more employment, they can as a first step appoint additional staff and workers to keep the offices like post offices, banks and certain important Government offices open on Saturdays and Sundays also. The public will greatly appreciate such a step.

While paying attention to increasing production and creating more wealth, we should not forget the need to reduce disparities and to provide minimum essential needs to one and all.

16

Salesmanship

Generally, a country's prosperity is assessed from the progress of its industrialisation. As the production increases with the multiplication of industries, the need for maintaining the quality of the product also becomes essential. Simultaneously competition also will grow. For the growth or even survival of any industry, the prompt sales of its products at the controlled or reasonable prices are very vital. Once the stocks of the product get accumulated, the industry becomes unviable, unprofitable and faces several other problems. Therefore the importance of salesmanship cannot be ignored in the context of growing competition.

But, often, there is a tendency to ignore this fact and due attention is not paid to equip the salesman with technical details of the products to enable him to do his job with skill and efficiency. We content ourselves by mobilising all our resources to increase production only. The days are gone, when in times of scarcity, anything pushed into the market was sold. Now, since there is a wide choice of the products available in the market, the customer subjects the product to thorough inspection and wants to be satisfied fully about its quality, usefulness and long term economy. Hence the salesman should be given sufficient training or instruction to gain enough knowledge to answer the queries of the customers and to illustrate the uses or special qualities of his product and to convince the customer that the choice of his product is most prudent and wise on his part.

Quite often, we ask the poor salesman in a fancy shop many questions about a newly arrived product and seek his advice. If the salesman is not prompt in convincing the customer about the things he is selling, the buyer may walk off. This may apply to any commodity, big or small – may be cement or steel, cars or cosmetics. When two cars of different makes or two pumps of different types are available in the market, much would depend on the skill of the salesman to influence the choice of the customer.

Similarly when choice of two products like steel and cement in the construction of a factory building or A.C. sheet and G.I. sheet in providing roofing over a building or cement and asphalt in constructing a road or mosaic flooring and plastic tile flooring (or marble) in the construction of a bungalow is open to a prospective customer, much would depend on the salesman's approach and his skill in explaining the good points and relative advantages of his product to the customer to get the final decision to his favour. If a salesman of cement does not know what proportion of cement and sand should be adopted for plastering work and how much strength the concrete is expected to develop in a prestressed concrete job, he would not be able to create a good market demand for his product.

The continued increase in production of cement brings in its wake enormous problems of marketing. This is all the more so, as other materials like plastic, P.V.C., bitumen, steel, glass are increasingly competing to edge out cement from some of the works traditionally being done with it. Hardly any start was made in the construction of ferrocement boats when plastic boats had started to be built. The great effort being made to persuade the authorities concerned to prefer concrete raods as against bituminous and other types of roads have yet to produce concrete results. This is because the propaganda work has reached only the fringe of the circle to be influenced. The salesman and sales promoters can do magnificient work by supplementing and carrying on this propaganda initiated in the interest of cement industry as well as the longterm national economy.

Intensive work of this kind, practical demonstrations, free technical assistance would help in persuading people to opt for concrete roads. Similarly, the advantages of cement based products like mosaic tiles concrete sinks, jallies, pipes, door and window frames, soil cement bricks etc. should be brought hom to one and all by the salesman who comes into intimate contact with the present and prospective users of cement.

Research

The salesman should keep abreast of all the latest cement based products coming into the market and should be well informed about the research and sales promotion work carried out by organisations like the Cement Research Institute, Cement Marketing Company, Cement Service Bureau, Concrete Association of India and Alokudyog Cement Service. They should also know something about light weight concrete, ferrocement, air entrained and cellular concrete and the like. Whenever they come across people who are unaware of the above but there is scope to use them in their works they should recommend the use of the above products which in turn will increase the consumption of cement.

Due to inadequate knowledge many builders use the cement in an improper way and complain about what they consider as defects such as rate of setting of cement, cracks in plastering or concrete, white patches formed at joints of the cement concrete or plastering works due to hydration and expulsion of freelime. Every time some complaints are received it would not be possible nor is necessary for an engineer or a chemist to meet the complainant. If the salesman is well trained, he would be able to attend to the complaints and satisfy the complainants if the cement is not defective. Where the complaints are more serious and beyond the capacity of the salesman to attend to, a Civil Engineer or a Chemist may be deputed to look into them.

Quality of Cement

Quality of much of the cement gets affected in transport or storage if proper care is not taken to prevent its exposure to dampness and moisture. The salesman or sales representatives should also know some important points about the correct method of storage of cement as mentioned below and from time to time they should check godowns of the stockists and set right any defective method followed by them.

The roof of the godown in which cement is to be stored should be ensured to be completely leak proof. The doors and windows should be in good condition so as not to allow water to penetrate through them when they are closed. The walls of the building should have a good plastering on both sides so as to render the walls impervious. The basement of the building should be raised well above the road level or the surrounding ground level to prevent the possible flow of surface water into the godown. It is advisable that the floor of the godown is made up of cement concrete to prevent seepage of ground water inside the room.

Cement should not be stacked directly on the floor of the godown. A raised platform should be made out of wooden sleepers and timber scantlings to a height of at least 6" above floor level. In areas where the rainfall is very heavy a water proof layer like a tarpaulin may be provided over the wooden platform. Cement bags should be stacked on such a platform to prevent clodding of cement due to dampness in the floor.

Cement bags should be stacked in such a manner that in

each vertical stack there are not more than 10 bags. However, if the time of storage is short, say not exceeding 10 days, the vertical stack may contain upto 15 bags. The bags should be stacked flat lying on their larger side i.e. they should not be kept erect on their ends.

It is advisable to leave a space of about one foot between the wall face and the cement stack as a precaution against possible damage of cement due to dampness in the walls.

The doors and windows should be well fastened to prevent them from accidentally opening in heavy gales accompanying rain.

The stacking of cement should be so arranged as to dispose of the cement in the same order in which it is received i.e. the cement received in an earlier consignment must be disposed of before the next arrivals. This has to be ensured as otherwise the cement may deteriorate owing to long storage.

Types of Cement

Salesman should be given a good knowledge about the various types of cement like the Pozzolana cement, masonry cement, hydrophobic cement, oil well cement, quick setting cement, high alumina cement, rapid hardening cement, white cement etc. They should also know something about the admixtures for retarding or quickening the setting process, or for rendering cement water proof, wear resistant etc. like "ceco", "accoproof", "ritarax", "cemproof". A knowledge of the above will enable a salesman to render useful help to his customers by suitably advising the type of cement or admixture that could be used in particular circumstances. Thereby the customer will have greater confidence in the salesman and turn to him for his guidance whenever he faces a construction difficulty where cement or cement based products could profitably be used.

Thus it is highly advisable that a special training be given to all recruits as salesmen or representatives with a view to equipping them with the above type of fundamentals which could greatly help in making their work easy and successful. Even stockists of cement should have basic knowledge of the use of cement.

Now-a-days cement salesmen are considered as non-technical personnel. It is believed by many that it is enough for a salesman if he knows something about the sales tax, freight pool contribution, excise, transport and if he has capacity to tour or meet people and appeal to them to use their cement. But this is not enough. If we take the example of mechanical equipment like, lathes, drilling machines, jaw crushers and other tools, highly qualified engineers or otherwise well trained personnel are appointed to look after sales and sales promotion work.

They are thorough with the details of the components of the machines they are required to sell. They also know as to where they could be recommended and what are their special advantages over other similar machines. Cement industry also may follow suit by equipping the salesman with knowledge about the latest developments in the uses of cement so that they could in turn carry on intensive propaganda work to increase the sales of cement and thereby contribute their mite to put on 'Terra firma' the plans and programmes of further expansion of the cement industry.

These suggestions given with reference to the cement industry would apply to the other industries as well.

17

Unjust Treatment of Certain Services

It is a well known fact that there is a wide disparity in the employment/promotion opportunities, salary and perks, powers, privileges and responsibilities between various services. Unless this is set right, the people will feel dissatisfied. A case study is given below by highlighting the position of civil engineers in the industry, to drive home this point.

The problems encountered by a Civil Engineer in the execution of an industrial project are many and most intricate. Most of those problems emanate from the fact that he has to shoulder heavy responsibilities with practically no powers, worth-mentioning. Hierarchy wise, he is placed at a far lower position than his counterparts with equal qualification and experience in other disciplines. The present trend of the Management thinking forecloses any possibility of a civil engineer being promoted to a commensurate position within the department or a transfer to another department enlarging his responsibilities beyond civil engineering functions. More often than not, people having no knowledge of civil engineering work will interfere with the day-to-day construction work, playing havoc on the quality and throwing to the winds the basic norms and specifications that are required to be followed. If, in the process, satisfactory results are achieved by any chance, the credit for this is promptly cornered by them. But, if anything goes wrong, the blame is put at the door of the poor civil engineer. In short, the lot of a civil engineer working in an industry is most unenviable.

A few problems of the above nature are recounted below, without mentioning the names of the projects where they have occurred:

Programme for work

A project in which more than 50,000 Cu.m. of controlled concrete was to be laid and some of the structures were going to a height of 80 metres above ground level was originally programmed for completion in 24 months. But later, some delays occurred in the finalisatin of the machinery and process detailing. The management was keen on sticking to the original date of commissioning of the plant. The consultants held discussions with the machinery suppliers and erectors and found that there was no scope for reducing the time allotted to them in the project. Therefore, without even consulting the civil engineers, the time for civil engineering work was cut down to 18 months. Subsequently, some more delay occurred owing to some problems regarding financing of the project. Again this loss of time was sought to be made up by reducing the time given for civil engineering work to 15 months in an arbitrary and peremptory manner. Ultimately, the project was completed in a record time of 22 months, thanks to excellent work of an able and enterprising civil engineering department and the sincere and pains-taking efforts of the civil engineering contractors. But some people at the helm at the project site had tried to hood-wink the management about the enormous delays in the work of other departments and tried to put the blame for the delay in the commissioning of the plant, on the Civil engineers. The management could see for themselves the time taken for the construction work in similar neighbouring projects. But they would not do so.

Delay due to rains and labour problems

During the course of the construction, a delay of 1½ months occurred owing to unprecedented rains in two consecutive rainy seasons and a strike by the construction labour for a week. But the people with no civil engineering back-ground who were in overall charge of the project would not see reason and allow any extension of time for the civil engineering work.

Delay in receipt of drawings

The drawings for the civil engineering work are invariably delayed by the consultants as they in turn would not have received the necessary data from the machinery suppliers for incorporation in the drawings. At times, the contractors' resources will be kept idle for want of drawings. Some times, the drawings for several works will be released simultaneously causing considerable strain on the contractors' resources. The people at the helm of the project question the civil engineers and the contractors as to how much time a structure may take for completion. If they indicate that the structure would take 12 months, they will be cross examined and coerced to agree to complete within 9 months. They would further expect that it is enough if the drawings are released exactly 9 months before the stipulated date of completion. The people in-charge fail to note that delays could happen due to unforeseen constructional details, as the earlier programmes were furnished on the basis of schematic or general arrangement drawings in the absence of detailed drawings. Further, if the drawings of each work are given in this manner, each work will become a critical work.

The people in-charge often meddle with civil engineering drawings, changing the location of partition walls, windows, doors and the elevation features in the name of functional requirement or economy, thus causing a lot of confusion. They expect all the missing details in the drawings to be supplemented by the civil engineers, thinking that such work is so simple. But what is to be noted is that these people cannot think of any changes in the machinery, electrical equipment and instrumentation although they are supposed to be experts in those fields.

If a drawing is received on a Saturday evening, these people in-charge of the project want the work to be commenced on Sunday morning, if not Saturday evening itself. This kind of haste on the part of the people in-charge of the project is unfortunately passing for dynamism. In a few cases, it is observed that the buildings so completed in haste are kept unused for several months after handing over.

Impatience

If at the depth shown in the drawing for laying a foundation, soft strata is encountered and a little more excavation is suggested by the civil engineers the project management is annoyed and infuriated and accuse that the civil engineers are not bold. They will make no secret of their impatience and cross examine the civil engineers as to what might happen to the structure, if founded on the soft strata.

Scant regard for norms of construction

In their impetuosity, these people advise the premature stripping of the shuttering for R.C. beams, slabs and the like with the wrong notion that they are thereby expediting the progress of work. These people never realise the enormity of the risk that is being taken in doing so. They appear to be blissfully ignorant of the consequences of a possible failure of the structure. The time required for rectification in the event of a failure will be far more than the extra time that might be required in carrying out the work in a neat and systematic manner. These people have scant regard for other specifications like construction joints, curing, compaction, size of aggregates, etc.

Contractors take advantage

The contractors take full advantage of such conditions at a project site. They often go to these impetuous people in charge of the project, if permission is not given by the civil engineers for concreting on account of defects noticed in the shuttering or reinforcement or quality of aggregates. In a surly manner, these people will question their civil engineers as to why they have not checked these things even while the work was being done. Their attitude of finding fault with the civil engineers instead of taking the contractors to task for their faulty work will only result in frustration and at times to acquiescence. The engineers will be afraid of stopping the work of a contractor even if they are not satisfied with the way the work is being done. There are instances galore of contractors starting the concreting works even before the reinforcement is fully tied or the shuttering is properly levelled and joints sealed.

Frivolous remarks

Nearly 220 tonnes of steel was used in the raft foundation for a silo of an internal diameter of 18 m. and a height of 80 metres above ground level. The people in-charge started making frivolous remarks that such a huge quantity of steel is not required and the consultants' design was very much on the safe side. Similar remarks are made about depth of a foundation, size of a column or a beam or a machine foundation without having any idea about the loads coming on those structures. But the same people never care to check whether the H.P. of a motor recommended by the consultant/process collaborator is on the high side or a gear box and shaft of a machine are designed with too much of a factor of safety, although they owe their positions to their possession of a degree in Electrical or Mechanical engineering.

Premature loading of structures

These people turn a deaf ear to the objections raised by civil engineers for prematurely loading the concrete structures. After placing the machine in position, the commissioning may be delayed for months for want of a few accessories. At times the need for the accessories will be realised after almost the entire erection work is completed. But they would not listen to civil engineers and wait for a few more days for the structure to attain the designed strength before loading it.

The time taken for the erection of a machine may exceed all their estimates and programmes by several weeks. But once it is ready, even if it is midnight, they want the grouting work to be taken up immediately. If they indicate beforehand as to when the grouting work is required to be done, arrangements could be made and people kept ready for doing this work. But in the absence of such fore-warning, organising work at short notice will become well-neigh impossible and the civil engineers will be blamed for the so called delay of a few hours without any justification what-so-ever. Another point to be noted is that the contractors will be disbanding their organisation by the time the grouting work is taken up and they will not be showing sufficient interest in carrying out grouting work, promptly. It will be a good idea if the machinery suppliers/erectors are given the responsibility for grouting the machines.

Deletion of certain items from the contract

A contractor should be allowed to carry out the entire work as per his contract. Even if a few items were not foreseen at the time of the preparation of tender schedules, the contractor should be asked to carry out those items for proper coordination. However, the people in-charge of the project tend to complicate issues by either withdrawing a portion of the work from the original contract or introducing other contractors for doing new items of work. In one contract, there was an item for transporting surplus earth from the various work sites. But the persons in-charge of the project said that some earth-moving equipment was ordered and would be coming shortly and that equipment could be deployed for the clearance of earth. Therefore the contractor started piling up heaps of earth near the various work sites. The place became shabby and there was absolutely no space for movement around the structures. There was considerable delay in the delivery of the earth-moving equipment. On receipt, they found some parts missing in the equipment. Finally, when they were got ready, it was found that the heaps of earth were inaccessible because of the machinery for erection and other materials lying alround the heaps. A portion of the earth only could be removed with great difficulty. Because of the site conditions, the out-turn of the machinery was only a fraction of its rated capacity. During this period the work for which the equipment was bought was badly delayed. It has never occurred to them that the diesel, operator's wages, wear and tear and depreciation would amount to more than the amount that would have been paid to the contractor. In the instance quoted here, the contractor was asked to remove the balance quantity of earth that could not be removed by the earth-moving equipment. As there was no clear-cut account as to how much earth was transported departmentally, there was utter confusion in assessing the quantity of earth transported by the contractor.

In the housing colony of more than 200 houses built simultaneously with the plant buildings, the people incharge of the project deleted the item of water proofing of the roofs, much against the advice of civil engineers in order to save a few lakhs of rupees in the project cost. In the next rainy season these people realised their folly and sanctioned money for water-proofing the roofs but not before some damage was caused to the interior decoration and bitter criticism voiced by the occupants of the houses about the leaks that were noticed here and there. It is strange that these people cannot cut down the cost of machinery and equipment. Usually, they yield to the terms dictated by machinery suppliers and process collaborators, mutely and helplessly.

Miscellaneous construction work

In addition to the works covered by the main contract,

several ancillary ;building works are required to be carried out by the civil engineers. For each of these works, the department is required to prepare drawings, estimates, tender schedules etc. and when the construction is in progress, it is also responsible for the supervision work. Although this increases the work load of the department which is always under-staffed, the department is not given any importance at all. Very often fresh proposals for construction work are required to be put up with all the relevant details only to be shelved by the management. Until a definite decision is taken to carry out a work, detailed drawings and estimates should not be asked for. But the pleas of civil engineers in this regard are never heeded.

The management expects the civil engineers to know A to Z in civil engineering whereas they are reconciled to the fact that a mechanical engineer or an electrical engineer might have knowledge only in a very limited sphere. A thousand faults in machinery erection or process control are tolerated as being quite normal or may not come to light but not a minor fault in the construction work.

Pivotal role of civil engineers

In any industrial project, the civil engineering department plays a key role. Whereas the machines are made in factories and sent to site for erection, the entire construction of civil engineering structures is done at the site under the constant supervision of civil engineers. Civil engineers are expected to know the specifications and the construction techniques. A lot of planning and co-ordination and a high degree of administrative ability are called for in managing a large construction work successfully. Ability to cut the avoidable delays, fix realistic programmes, give clarifications in work, hold review meetings, handle correspondence and maintain good relations with contractors, consultants and other departments of the project, is a prime requisite of the civil engineer heading the department. But even with all these qualities, a civil engineer is never considered as eligible for promotion to higher positions in the industries.

During the course of the project implementation, for more than half the time initially, people outside the civil engineering department will have no work at all. During the remaining period also, they sorely depend upon the machinery suppliers and process collaborators for the erection of the machinery and commissioning. Indeed many of these people admit that they were no better than trainees in the project. But inspite of these facts, the people in these departments rise fast in their careers and are given powers to meddle with civil engineering. It is unfortunate that it is believed that any body belonging to any department, say, Mechanical, Electrical, Accounts, Administration or Sales could go to top positions but not civil engineers. The civil engineers are considered fit for civil engineering work only. Even during the peak-work period when civil engineers will be toiling hard, some people will be lamenting that once the buildings are completed, the civil engineers will not have much work. But they would not think of the people who were idle and without work right at that moment. Even when the plant is commissioned, the people of the other departments would not have half the work that the civil engineers are required to do during the project stage. After the completion of the project too, the miscellaneous constructions, additions and alterations to buildings and maintenance work will keep the civil engineers as busy as the plant engineers.

Corrective measures

To correct this anamoly and to render justice to civil engineers, it is high time that the industries did a rethinking on the policy of promotions to top positions. Civil engineers must be treated on par with engineers and officers in other departments. Civil engineering work should be left to the charge of civil engineers and the day-to-day work should not be interfered with. Civil engineering staff during the project implementation stage should be given perks and facilities which are made available to personnel of equal cadre after the project is commissioned. Civil engineers with experience and talents should be considered for promotion to higher administrative and managerial positions without keeping them stagnant.

These steps will help in greatly boosting the morale of the civil engineersworking in the industries and improve the efficiency of the civil engineering departments.

Conclusion

Like the civil engineers in the industries, there are some aggrieved sections of the employees in almost all the departments of the Government, public sector companies, private sector companies etc. Unless their grievances are looked into and a reasonable solution found to their satisfaction, they will continue to sulk at the step-motherly treatment meted out to them. Such conditions may not be conducive to the smooth and efficient functioning of the Department/Company.

18

Rules and Bureaucracy

The general impression in the minds of the people is that the disposal of papers/files is very slow in the Government offices. Almost every one who had visited a Government office for an application to be processed or a petition to be approved or a license to be granted or a clarification about a circular/rule/notification etc. would have an anecdote or a story to tell as to how he had been made to run from pillar to post and how much time he had to waste before getting his work done.

Some people say that the staff and officers reach their offices late in the morning and stop their work well before the scheduled closing time. In addition, they spend much more than the allotted time for lunch, tea etc. They also waste quite a lot of time in chatting with friends and going hither and thither.

Some others complain that many of them are lazy and careless. A few of them also tell that unless money is paid they would not attend to their papers even if they are of a routine nature.

It may be of interest to note that such an impression is created largely due to the attitude of about 35% of the Government employees only. There are many people in the Government service who are quite sincere in their work. Quite a few of them are even responsive and helpful to the public. However, such people too are unable to expedite the disposal of the papers/files due to certain rigid bureaucratic rules.

It should be understood that the basic nature of a person remains the same wherever he/she may be employed. But, in a private company, a person with an unreasonable attitude will try to mend his/her ways in order to adjust himself/herself to the work culture of the company. An employee failing to do so may face the prospect of being thrown out of his/her job. A private company would never tolerate its image getting tarnished because of the brusque and unresponsive attitude of its employee. Moreover, the rules being more flexible in a private company, an employee cannot delay a matter for long, taking shelter under the rules, like an employee in a Government office. In a private company, an aggrieved party could expect redressal of his grievance with regard to an employee by meeting a person at the next higher level. In a Government office, this does not work as, more often than not, the superior officer would not like to intervene effectively.

Perhaps, an example or a case study would help the reader to understand the delays in the disposal of papers/files and attitudes of the staff and officers in Government offices. With this in view, the ordeal that a company representative had to pass through recently for getting an application approved in a Government Department is narrated here briefly.

It took two months for the application to be approved, in spite of his close follow-up from time to time. He found the under secretary non-chalant and totally ;unconcerned with the plight of the applicant. For the first two weeks, the application was not looked into as he was on leave. After another two weeks, he called for some information from the company, which was already available in his office. Thereby, another week was lost. After a good number of reminders over the next two weeks, he had sent the file to the Joint Secretary who had signed it within a day. The Under Secretary went on a tour for one week by the time the file returned to his office.

A formal letter approving the application was ready two months after its submission. As the company fixed a deadline for sending that letter, the company representative met the Under Secretary with a letter of authorisation for taking delivery of the letter in person. But, true to his nature, the Under Secretary asked him to meet him the next day. The Company Representative told him about the company's dire need of the paper urgently and requested for the delivery of the letter that day itself to enable him to send it by FAX/courier. Then, the Under Secretary called his Section Officer and scolded him for having given the information that the letter was sent to him for his signature already. He repeated several times that he was an honest man and would not like to work under pressure. One wonders whether "being honest" gives the right to anyone for tardiness!

Finally, after expressing his resentment for reminding him so many times, he gave the letter which, to the surprise of the Company Representative, was already signed by him! Was it for a sadistic pleasure that he had asked the Company Representative to meet him the next day, when the letter was already signed by him and ready for despatch?

During the course of this follow-up work, the Company Representative had met the Director who is above the Under Secretary. Although, he assured that he would not delay the paper in his office even for a minute when it came, he refused to speak with the Under Secretary to expedite the matter. The Company Representative found the Section Officer to be quite responsive and understanding. When approached and told about the urgency of the matter and the delay that has already taken place, he processed the paper and sent up the file to the Under Secretary immediately. However, a delay of one day resulted due to the absence of the Section Officer at one stage.

The Assistant in the Section told that according to the rules, the letter of approval could not be put up to the Under Secretary in the absence of the Section Officer!

It is high time that some measures are taken for improving the present system of working in the Government offices. To start with, perhaps the following steps could be taken.

(1) The staff and officers should be advised to be responsive to the people.

(2) They should be advised to be reasonably prompt in the disposal of papers/files. A time frame may be fixed for this purpose.

(3) They should understand that some one would telephone or meet them only when it is absolutely necessary and not to disturb them or to put pressure on them.

(4) Such long procedure like a letter/noting written by an Assistant having to pass through the Section Officer, Under Secretary and Director to the Joint Secretary for his approval may be cut short to some extent in order to speed up the disposal of files and to reduce the routine type of work load on the officers.

(5) If a clarification is required, the concerned person should be called by the officer for a discussion across the table instead of returning the file through the various levels stated above. For the file to pass through all these levels it takes a lot of time.

(6) Absence of a person should not be allowed to delay the disposal of papers/files unless it is absolutely unavoidable. Authorisation should be given to the person above or below his rank to sign the papers in his absence.

It may be appropriate to quote a few lines here from the valedictory address of the late L.K. Jha at the National Academy of Administration, Mussoorie on 19-7-85.

"Today, in each department, in addition to the levels existing in the past, there are Directors as well as Additional Secretaries. The trend is for the file to pass through each level. As a matter of administrative reform, the suggestion has been made that there should be level jumping.

One of the most unfortunate consequences of all these compexities is that every thing which requires to be done or cleared by the Government takes too much time. In consequence, things move slowly."

19

Importance of Proper Communications

One of the requirements for the efficiency of a Manager is his/her ability for crisp,clear and timely communications.

Very often we find some political leaders issuing denials of having made certain remarks or statements attributed to them in the newspaper reports. This could be happening either because the leaders have not expressed themselves clearly or the reporters have understood the leaders' words in a different way. In politics, such things are being viewed as of routine nature.

However, in management, if a Manager seems to have retracted on his statement, his subordinate staff will lose faith in him and his employers would have doubts about his reliability. Therefore, a Manager should be careful in choosing his words while giving an instruction to his subordinates and also while reporting to his employers.

Communications could be made orally or in writing. While the oral communications may be direct or through telephone, wireless etc. the written communications are usually in the form of a letter, a telegram, a telex, a fax etc. A communication through gestures also is resorted to once in a while due to the distance between the persons and nonavailability of instruments like a walkie talkie.

While making an oral communication, one should make sure that those receiving the communication have understood properly. For, many times, the communications are not understood because of the problems with regard to accent, pronounciation, language and inaudibility.

The following joke may perhaps illustrate the problem with regard to accent. Once, a person invited his friend for a "Bhajan" at his house on a particular day. The friend went to his house expecting to be given a dinner as the word "Bhajan" was pronounced as "Bhojan" while inviting him. But, he had to be content with participating in the Bhajan and returning home with empty stomach.

If a Manager speaks in English to an attender whose knowledge of English is only rudimentary the attender is quite likely to do something funny at times. A newly appointed Manager who preferred to speak in English in the office and also encoureged the staff to follow his example has called the attender one day and asked "Where is the Accounts Officer? Please call him". The attender replied, "Just get out, Sir". The Manager got angry on hearing such an unexpected reply. Just at that time, the Assistant Manager appeared on the scene and explained to the Manager that what the attender had meant to convey was that the Accounts Officer went out of office just a little while ago. The Manager had a good laugh and got used to such replies, later on.

Once, an employee transferred form Madras to Gurgaon contacted his Manager located at Delhi over telephone. The Manager asked him to wait for him at the Himalaya House at 3.00 P.M. for receiving further instructions. At the appointed time, the Manager went to the Himalaya House to meet the employee. Even by 5.00 P.M. the employee did not turn up at the venue. The Manager went back wondering as to why the employee did not reach the place. The next day, the employee again telephoned to the Manager and told him that he went to Gurgaon thinking that the Himalaya House was at Gurgaon. He apologised profusely for his mistake.

In this case, the Manager could have given his instruction more clearly making the employee understand that the place mentioned was in Delhi itself. Similarly, the employee too could have asked for the full address of the place where he was to meet the Manager without assuming that the place was at Gurgaon.

Some communications like this are between one person and another only. In some other cases, the communications may have to be coordinated between several parties located at different places.

Once a consultant at Delhi was asked by a Manager of a Company located at Calcutta to collect some money from the Company's local office at Delhi. The consultant went to the Delhi Office. But the Manager in Delhi office told the Consultant that he had not received any communications from his office at Calcutta. It is needless to tell how the Consultant would have felt.

In this case, the Manager in Calcutta should have ensured that his communication has reached the Manager in his Delhi Office by the time the Consultant was expected to go to his Delhi Office.

In certain cases, the delay in communication or the lack of coordination could prove to be too costly.

Once a person received a telex message saying that he should receive a guest of his company arriving from Bombay in the morning on the next day. As there were four flights arriving from Bombay in the morning from 8.00 A.M. to 12.00 Noon, he was at a loss to know by which of those flights that guest was arriving. If only the flight number and the time of arrival too were mentioned, in the message, the person would have been spared much of his trouble.

Suppose an important document was being sent by a courier from Madras asking the Company's representative in Delhi to submit it in the office of a Government Department the next day. In that case, soon after despatching the document, the office in Madras should send a message to the concerned person by telex, fax or by telephone giving details of the name of the courier service, despatch document number and when the document was to be submitted. This will facilitate the tracing of the documents in case there is delay in the delivery of the document by the courier service. Moreover, the person who has to submit the documents will keep himself free at that time. In the absence of such a message, the document might not reach the Government Department in time either because of delay in its delivery by the courier Service company or the non-avialability of the person who has to submit the paper to the Government Department.

20

Tips for Business Development and Improving Efficiency

Happily there is now a noticeable spurt in the construction activity all over the country. Usually, the construction activity is an index of the rate of development in the country. Government has given sanction for the construction of a large number of projects like thermal and hydel power plants, irrigation works, housing complexes, roads and bridges etc. Undoubtedly this is also an opportune time for many of the Civil Engineering construction companies to consolidate their business and also to expand the same. However, quite a few companies are either too conservative or too matter-of-fact in their functioning to derive any benefit from this favourable situation. They would not care to do a little introspection to improve their efficiency and to take necessary steps to expand their business.

A few tips given hereunder, if implemented, could perhaps yield very desirable results.

(1) Training the new recruits:

It should be ensured that the new recruits with little experience are trained properly in the first few months. This is required to mould them into proper form. With this kind of training, they will be able to learn to do their work in a neat and a systematic manner.

(2) Middle level Managers:

Experienced managers should be encouraged to work independantly as far as their day to day work is concerned. They should be able to take decisions without looking up to higher levels for approval at every stage. This is very essential not only for their own growth and streamlining the work but also for relieving the burden on the top managers.

(3) Top level Managers:

A well known management consultant has once told that the top managers who keep on telling about the pressure of work on them are found generally to spend more than half of their time in trivial matters on which their attention need not have been bestowed. If this time is saved, they could surely do more justice to the remaining work, which is more important. The top managers should content themselves with laying down the guide lines for work and reviewing the performance at various sites, periodically. Here is an interesting joke. A senior officer, John tells his junior, David, "Look, I am very reasonable. I believe in equitable sharing of work. Here, we have got two things, power and responsibility. I shall have power and you shall have responsibility". This attitude could prove detrimental to the morale of the staff.

(4) Modernisation:

To remain competitive, one has to change with times. One cannot afford to ignore the changes and improvements taking place in technology, methods of work, construction equipment and management techniques. For this, every company should depute at least 2 to 6 of their staff with the right aptitude and background to attend seminars, training courses and visit exhibitions and trade fairs within the country and abroad every year. This should not be viewed as an expenditure but as an investment.

(5) Aptitude of staff:

It is an accepted fact that different people can excel in

different fields depending upon their aptitudes. One who is very good in quantity surveying could prove to be a flop when he is asked to take over a construction site. One who is excellent in planning and monitoring may feel like a fish out of water if he is asked to be in charge of quality control. Thus, it is necessary to understand the aptitudes of the staff and to entrust to them such work in which they could display their talents, fully.

(6) Management information systems:

M.I.S. should be given due importance. All necesary data and reports must be sought from the different project sites. But, collection of superfluous or redundant information should be avoided. It is learnt that until a few years ago, the lists of all the air passengers were being sent to the Managing Director of Indian Air lines every day. Obviously, the M.D. would not have been interested in these lists. Nor would it have been possible for him to spare so much time to read the lengthy lists of those names. This practice was discontinued only when a management consultant had pointed out that this is not serving any purpose.

(7) Recruitment Policy:

Every company should keep the names of several candidates on its files for different kinds of posts. Particularly, when the company is tendering for a non traditional project as part of a diversification plan, it should advertise for the personnel likely to be required and keep the candidates with the right type of experience on waiting lists. The trasfer of staff from the company's traditional projects may not help as they would be lacking the kind of experience that is called for in the new project tendered for. It should be borne in mind that a candidate may not be available for employment, if he is called 9 months or one year after he is interviewed. Therefore, these lists must be updated by entering into correspondance with the interviewed candidates or calling new candidates for a fresh interview.

(8) Policies for growth:

The management should spell out clearly, the goals and policies in respect of the company's growth. For, if a company with a turnover of say, Rs. 60 crores sets its target for trebling its annual turnover with in a span of, say, 3 years the company should aim at bagging contracts with a value to the tune of 3 to 4 times of the value of the projected turnover. This would require a tremendous effort. Perhaps the company should enter into areas other than its traditional areas. For this, perhaps joint venture contracts with other companies having relevant experience in other areas may be required for the purpose of prequalification. The Company could try for foreign projects also very vigourously.

(9) Marketing:

Good marketing is the key to success of any plans for the growth of a company. At least, it is as important as the construction work in a project. In civil engineering construction companies, marketing or business development work requires personnel with techno-commercial skills. They should not only know about the civil engineering work and projects, but also have the abilities for establishing contacts with potential clients, gathering particulars and salient details of projects coming up in the near future and getting their companies recognised by the concerned authorities as competent to take up the projects and deliver the goods. No doubt, those who have read the now famous biography of the modern wizard of business management, IOCOCCA would be able to recall to their minds the importance that he has attached to marketing work in his industry. Marketing should be a continuous process and should be carried on always on sound lines. In these days, a lot of spade work is required in getting prequalified even in an area in which the company is already experienced.

A company should never become complacent and neglect marketing work, thinking that the order book is satisfactory after bagging one or two contracts. Unless, marketing work is given the importance that is its due, the price that a company may have to pay at a later date to have a respectable figure on its order book after the completion of one or two of its projects on hand, may prove to be too high.

The above points are no doubt very simple, but often neglected. The companies will do well to review the working procedures of the company periodically with an open mind, with the help of a management consultant, preferably.